NEVER GREATER SLAUGHTER

OSPREY
PUBLISHING

NEVER GREATER SLAUGHTER

BRUNANBURH AND
THE BIRTH OF ENGLAND

MICHAEL
LIVINGSTON

OSPREY PUBLISHING
Bloomsbury Publishing Plc
Kemp House, Chawley Park, Cumnor Hill, Oxford OX2 9PH, UK
29 Earlsfort Terrace, Dublin 2, Ireland
1385 Broadway, 5th Floor, New York, NY 10018, USA
E-mail: info@ospreypublishing.com
www.ospreypublishing.com

OSPREY is a trademark of Osprey Publishing Ltd

First published in Great Britain in 2021

ISBN: HB 978 1 4728 4937 3; PB 978 1 4728 4938 0; eBook 978 1 4728 4927 4;
ePDF 978 1 4728 4928 1; XML 978 1 4728 4929 8

21 22 23 24 25   10 9 8 7 6 5 43 2 1

Foreword © Bernard Cornwell
Maps by www.bounford.com
Index by Sharon Redmayne

Typeset by Deanta Global Publishing Services, Chennai, India
Printed and bound in Great Britain by CPI (Group) UK Ltd, Croydon, CR0 4YY

Contents

Foreword

By Bernard Cornwell

I suspect that if you ask people about battles fought on British soil they will suggest a few: Hastings, Bannockburn, Bosworth Field, Edgehill, and the Battle of Britain. Maybe they will remember Towton, Flodden, or Naseby, but very few people will add Brunanburh to their list of famous British battles.

Perhaps that's not surprising. It happened long ago, in AD 937, and over the centuries it became forgotten to the extent that no one was even sure where Brunanburh was. Yet perhaps no battle was so important to the shaping of Britain. As Michael Livingston wrote in his magnificent *The Battle of Brunanburh: A Casebook*, 'The men who fought and died on that field forged a political map of the future that remains with us today.'[1] That makes Brunanburh as significant an engagement as the battle of Yorktown in 1781 and, just as Yorktown established the existence of a United States of America, so Brunanburh sealed the creation of England.

Yet, strangely, the people of England largely forgot Brunanburh. For a time after 937 it was an extraordinarily famous battle, described in chronicles across Christendom, celebrated in poems and songs, and always remembered as a terrible event marked with massive slaughter. The *Anglo-Saxon Chronicle*, usually a dry catalogue of events, broke into verse to describe the battle, and this book takes its title from that poem. The language is the English of the time:

> Ne wearð wæl mare
> on þis eiglande,   æfre gieta

folces gefylled   beforan þissum
sweordes ecgum

> Never greater slaughter
> Was there on this island,   never as many
> Folk felled   before this
> By the swords' edges.[2]

Brunanburh was recognized as a crucial and appalling event, and as a battle that had consequence, just as Hastings would have. Yet, amazingly, the English forgot where the battle was fought. Names change over time. Mameceaster became Manchester, Snotengaham became Nottingham. It's a natural process and Brunanburh, wherever it was, went through the same changes until folk forgot the original name and, in the process, even managed to forget the famous battle that had been fought there. Over the years there have been myriad suggestions about where the battle was fought, ranging from the Solway Firth to County Durham, from Yorkshire to Cheshire, but it is only recently that archaeologists have discovered broken weapons that point towards the Wirral. Even those discoveries will probably not end the controversy, but having visited the site and talked to the archaeologists I am convinced we at last know where Brunanburh took place. If you happen to be driving the M53 towards Birkenhead then look to your left between Exits Four and Three, and there it is! The lost battlefield of Brunanburh.

So we now know, or think we know, where the battle was fought, and we know who fought there. On one side were the English, and on the other was an alliance of their enemies led by Anlaf, a famous Viking chieftain who had carved out a kingdom in Ireland and now claimed the kingship of Northumbria. He was allied with other Vikings and with Constantine, king of the Scots. They went to the Wirral with one aim: to end forever the power of the English.

The English! Who were they? The very word was unusual in the tenth century because the concept was fairly new. As Michael Livingston recounts so well in this book, the island of Britain had been invaded by tribes from what is now Germany. There were Angles, Saxons, and Jutes, who took over British land and forced the native Britons either north into southern Scotland, west into Wales and Cornwall, or south across the channel to Brittany. Those invading tribes formed seven kingdoms that eventually became four, and though they fought each other they shared a common language. They were related, they were alike to each other, they were Christians, and King Alfred of Wessex, the southernmost kingdom, had a vision of uniting them. That dream of a united Anglo-Saxon kingdom was in jeopardy because there were new and terrifying invaders, the pagan Vikings, who wanted to make their own kingdoms in Britain, and the Vikings swiftly conquered most of the northern and eastern land held by the Anglo-Saxons. Yet Alfred's dream of a united country lived on past his death and, little by little, the Anglo-Saxons reconquered much Viking territory until, shortly before Brunanburh, Alfred's grandson, King Athelstan, was the monarch of what had been Wessex, Mercia, and East Anglia. Only one Anglo-Saxon kingdom, Northumbria, remained under Viking rule.

The British Isles were a political mess in the early tenth century. There were at least a dozen kings, all eager for more land and ready to fight for it. Ireland was divided between the native Irish and the Norsemen who had captured much of the best land and who now, under Anlaf, claimed Northumbria. There were kings in Wales, ever mindful that the Angles and Saxons had conquered their ancestral lands. There were kings in Scotland, and all those people, Britons, Scots, and Norsemen, were aware that the strongest king was Athelstan of Wessex who now ruled a vast territory in southern Britain and who claimed the presumptuous title of *monarchus totius britanniae*, the monarch of all Britain. Athelstan also claimed Northumbria and, if he succeeded in capturing that swathe of northern land, he would become even more powerful, and so the northern kings, those in what is now Ireland and Scotland, combined to stop him. If Athelstan could be defeated then Saxon power might be broken forever.

Anlaf had a claim to the throne of Northumbria so his motive for going to war was to claim that throne which would add a great slice of rich territory to his Irish kingdom. Constantine, a Christian, probably did not want a Viking pagan on his southern frontier, but nor did he want the Saxons there. Athelstan had humiliated

Constantine in AD 934 by invading Scotland and leading his army to the northernmost tip of Constantine's land. Both Constantine and the Vikings feared Athelstan's power, knowing that he would dominate Britain unless he was destroyed. And so the allies invaded, and the two armies met at Brunanburh. Athelstan's forces won the battle and Northumbria became a part of Athelstan's kingdom and so a country called England was born on that terrible field.

And it was terrible. The basic concept of battle in those days was the clash of shield-walls, and to win a battle the enemy's shield-wall had to be broken. A shield-wall is just that, a long line of big ironbound willow shields carried by armoured warriors who have swords, spears, and axes. An attacking force would throw spears and shoot arrows at the opposing shield-wall, but to break it men had to get close, very close. Anglo-Saxon poetry often describes the horror of the shield-wall fight. Shields would clash against enemy shields, and then the warriors would hack and thrust at each other, trying to open a gap between the shields. If they killed an enemy in the front rank then there were four or five other ranks behind, all with their shields and weapons, all of which had to be broken. It was brutal close-quarter work with your enemy an arm's length away. If a shield-wall did break then it became worse because the defeated warriors would try to flee and then be cut down by their pursuers. We know this happened at Brunanburh because the poem in the *Anglo-Saxon Chronicle* tells us 'ymbe Brunanburh, bord-weall clufon' – 'near Brunanburh they split the shield-wall' – and the poem tells how Athelstan's victorious army pursued the beaten Scots and Vikings and killed them mercilessly.[3] Never greater slaughter was there on this island.

It truly was a memorable and crucial battle, and it is strange that it was eventually forgotten and that the English, who owe their very nation to the victory Athelstan won at Brunanburh, even forgot where the battle had been fought. No one has done more than Michael Livingston to revive memories of the battle, and now, just as he predicted, we can be almost certain that the great slaughter took place on the Wirral. It is ironic that an American has become the foremost interpreter of Brunanburh, England's battle, but if you want to know why it was fought, how it was fought and where it was fought, you could not hope for a better guide.

Preface

Late in 937, three armies met in a place they called Brunanburh. On one side stood the shield-wall of the expanding kingdom of the English. On the other side stood a remarkable alliance of rival kings – one of them a Viking from across the sea – who had come together to destroy them once and for all. The stakes were no less than the survival of the dream that would become England.

The violence shocked a violent age. Brunanburh may not have the fame of Hastings, Crécy, or Agincourt today, but those later battles, also fought for England, would not exist were it not for the blood spilled at Brunanburh. Generations afterwards it was still famous enough to need no name. It was called, quite simply, the 'great battle'.

And for centuries, its location has been lost.

Today, an extraordinary effort, uniting enthusiasts, historians, archaeologists, linguists, and other researchers – amateurs and professionals, experienced and inexperienced alike – may well be on the road to finding the site of the long-lost battle of Brunanburh, over a thousand years after its bloodied fields made history.

This book will tell the story of this remarkable work. It will also tell the story of why and how the battle happened. Most importantly, this book will tell the story of the men who fought and died at Brunanburh, and how much this forgotten struggle can tell us about who we are and how we relate to our past.

A QUICK WORD ABOUT HISTORY

History isn't facts.

History *relies* on facts, but it's bigger than the facts themselves.

The past is, by definition, over and done. What happened happened, we cannot change it, and there are, as a result, very real facts about our past. Yet one of the first problems in writing history is that we cannot access *all* the facts of a given moment, much less the totality of the past event from which they are made.

Imagine you saw a car accident. People were hurt. An investigation gets underway. Your perspective as an eyewitness to the event will, quite obviously, be enormously valuable. What you saw could provide the essential facts, the critical information that allows the investigators to understand what happened. But you won't be the only source of information for the investigators, and thank goodness! Because even though you were an eyewitness – indeed, *because* you were an eyewitness – your understanding of the accident will be limited. You only saw the accident through the lens of your individual perspective: from where you were standing, from the way you were facing, from the time that you looked to the time you looked away. Even worse, how you remember what you witnessed – how your brain creates its facts – depends a great deal on your own life and experiences. The car enthusiast and someone who has never seen an automobile will remember the event in very different ways. For this reason investigators will talk not just to you but to every witness they can find. They'll gather every scrap of information possible – tyre marks, video footage, anything they can get their hands on – and sift through it all to figure out what explanation best fits all the evidence they were able to find. They will then write up a report stating what they think happened.

If everyone agrees on the findings of our hypothetical investigators, we might call this report 'the truth'. But – and this is the important bit – the report on what happened isn't actually what happened. Not really. It's a *story* of the event, reflecting the most probable logical explanation of the known facts. Like a scientific hypothesis, the report will no longer be accepted as reflecting what happened if new information is discovered that invalidates the accepted story.

So it is with historians, who do much the same thing. Only instead of accidents, we investigate the past.

Most people understand history as the kind of work you currently have in your hands: the story of the past, the report. But this is only the last stage of a long sequence of labour that happens behind the scenes as women and men do the investigative job of finding facts, sifting them, coming up with a probable explanation, testing it, and then figuring out how best to present it as a (hopefully!) compelling story. At this last stage, like weavers forming the pattern of a tapestry, we create history by strategically moving the thread of our chosen narrative in and out through the threads of a million possible facts on the loom. Some of these facts will be known, but a great many will be, through the passage of time, unknowable: not only because some things are simply lost, but also because people actively choose which facts they preserve, and thus which stories can get told. Worse, because human beings have *always* chosen the facts that suit their needs and have *always* woven their own stories out of them, we must also contend with the problem that the witnesses to our past – the sources for our always-too-few facts – are not just biased to one degree or another, but they could also, quite simply, be lying.

As they go about this investigative work, historians must remain keenly aware of not only the many limitations of the sources they are using but also the limitations that they themselves have. Like the automotive awareness of our hypothetical eyewitness – who, you'll remember, only saw what they could see and understood what they could understand – historians carry into any investigation the limitations of their own lives, educations, and experiences. Those interested in telling the story of what happened in our past must therefore work hard to account for our own biases, and set aside – as far as possible – our preconceptions in order to tell what seems the best story of past events we cannot experience ourselves.

This is all, to put it mildly, hard.

This is not a historical methodologies textbook. There is neither the time nor the room to deep-dive on the varied procedures that modern historians use to sift through the available facts and find what seems the most likely truth of the story being told. But Brunanburh provides an excellent example of how all these theoretical problems meet the practical reality. To tell a history of Brunanburh, it's necessary to choose a story of Brunanburh.

There is an English Brunanburh. A Scottish Brunanburh. A Viking Brunanburh. A Welsh Brunanburh. A hard-to-access-but-equally-real Hebridean Brunanburh. And these categories break down even further: the story of Brunanburh as told from the perspective of Egil Skallagrimson is a Viking Brunanburh, but as someone who fought under the English king his would be a different story of the battle than those of the Vikings who were enemies of the English in the fight. And certainly the story of Brunanburh from the English king's point of view is quite different from the story as seen through the eyes of a farmer pressed into service for him.

The traditional history of Brunanburh is without doubt the story as seen through the lens of the English monarchy: how the battle furthered King Athelstan's aims and the march towards English superiority in England. To some degree, I have already adopted this story in choosing the title of this book: not only is 'never greater slaughter' how the most famous and very pro-English source described the amount of the enemy dead, but my subtitle focus on England's birth likewise supports this traditional point of view.

Nevertheless, the story of Brunanburh I will tell situates the battle against the backdrop of a century of conflict between multiple expansionist powers vying to control the future of Britain: particularly the Vikings and the English. This story highlights the military and political history of the period. If you want the story of Athelstan's glory, you will get it here. But I also want to show how it affected men and women who didn't wear crowns – and how the outcome wasn't written in the stars. Battles are inherently risky, and Brunanburh was a close-fought thing. Had the scales of war tipped even slightly the other way then the history of the battle, and indeed of Britain itself, would have been very different.

NAMES IN THIS BOOK

Already in these first pages I have used several words that are so familiar that they might not have received a second glance. *England. The English. Viking.* Despite their seeming simplicity, these words (and so many more) are enmeshed in complex histories. The truth is that their meanings are disputed, and even their casual use can have power and consequence. It will be important for me to explain what I mean when I use them – and why I feel I need to use them – as we move through the book. At the outset, however, there are just a few to get straight.

England and the *English*. Geographically, England is today that part of the United Kingdom that joins with Scotland and Wales to encompass the island of Great Britain. These modern political boundaries do not map well to the time period examined in this book. So I'll be using the words *England* and *English* to refer to those lands and peoples who were likely to identify themselves as having a common culture with the Angles, Saxons, Jutes, Myrgings, and other Germanic-speaking groups that had migrated to Great Britain after the Roman Empire had begun to change (a complex story that will be covered in due course!).

Anglo-Saxon. Historically speaking, this has been a common term for what I'm calling *England* and the *English*. I have used it myself in other books and articles. Increasingly, however, this term has been co-opted by right-wing groups who use it to create a racial identity within history that they then weaponize in present politics. This co-option is wrong, and while I don't like the idea of giving ground to racists who misuse historical terminology, the truth is that little at all is lost in shifting to the more generalized terms connected to England. That said, I will still on occasion use the term *Anglo-Saxon* – meaning the English – where doing so helps avoid confusion. I also have no intention of forcing a name-change to those works that have long had the older term attached to them, like the *Anglo-Saxon Chronicle*, an important source of information that will appear often in these pages.

Viking. The word *viking* is a verb, referring to foreign travel and raiding engaged in by people connected to Scandinavian culture, often using an arm of the sea, or *vik*. Those who engaged in viking came to be known as Vikings, but there remains intense academic debate over the degree to which this noun is a lasting identity. If a Viking sea-raid evolved into a farming settlement with hearth and home, are the raiders-turned-settlers no longer Vikings? It's a question that cuts to the heart of ethnic and cultural identities, and one that I cannot answer here. I will instead say that, for the purposes of this book, a Viking is simply someone who identifies with Scandinavian culture – including modern Denmark – 'active outside of Scandinavia'.[1]

Personal names can also be problematic. I have named the man who led the Vikings at Brunanburh using the Old English form of his name, Anlaf, rather than the Norse (Óláfr), Gaelic (Amhlaoibh), or Latin (Anlavus). While this choice could be seen as charged with political or cultural significance, it is driven solely by my desire to produce the most readable, accessible text possible – just as it is in my naming the English king Athelstan rather than the more correct Æþelstan.

Here and there throughout this book, you'll see words placed in italics – for example, the word *England* above. In these cases so far, this is done in order to highlight that I am talking about the word as a word. In other cases to come, however, it can also be done in order to show that a word is being left in its original, untranslated form – either because we don't know how to translate it or because I will be discussing just how to translate it later in the text.

KEY REFERENCES

The book will refer to specific scholars and specific research where necessary – particularly references to vital source materials – but endnotes will be kept to a minimum in order to keep the story moving along.

There will be a suggested reading list at the end of the book, but I need to highlight one particular volume up front. *The Battle of Brunanburh: A Casebook*, for which I served as general editor when it was published in 2011, collects most of the primary documents directly related to the battle of Brunanburh, so it will be frequently referenced herein. These references will be given in the format '*Brunanburh Casebook*, 2.12', representing the item number of the used source, followed by the exact line number or numbers of the English translation being utilized (for those who read them, the *Brunanburh Casebook* also provides original language texts on the facing pages). It is important for me to note here – and this will become even clearer as our story proceeds – that while my name may appear on the cover of this book, the work within is the result of an amazing international team of researchers. They and their work will be individually mentioned in due course, but I wanted to acknowledge them in total: I could not have reached this point without them.

For those sources not in the *Brunanburh Casebook*, I have translated them myself unless otherwise noted.

A NOTE ON DATES

Because *Anno Domini* dating (BC/AD) is inherently religious, many writers will opt to replace it with what's called Common Era dating (BCE/CE) in order to move history off a traditionally Christian axis. While I see the point in principle, Common Era does not achieve such a change. Indeed, rather than removing that religious axis, it merely hides it. Between these options, therefore, I've chosen the honest (and also more familiar to most readers) BC/AD dating.

If this offends, I am sorry – but I also offer up the solace that the Christian monks who devised the system so completely botched their calculations that it isn't at all accurate to what they were trying to achieve.

List of Illustrations

Fig. 14: A charter from November 931 in which Athelstan granted lands to a nobleman named Wulfgar. (© British Library Board. All Rights Reserved / Bridgeman Images)

Fig. 15: The Overchurch Runestone. (Williamson Art Gallery & Museum, Birkenhead; Wirral Museums Service)

Fig. 16: John Speed's 1611 map of the Wirral. (Stanford University Libraries, CC0 1.0)

Fig. 17: A painting by Charles Arthur Cox showing Wallasey Pool. (Williamson Art Gallery & Museum, Birkenhead; Wirral Museums Service)

Fig. 18: The remains of Skuldelev 1. (DEA / G. DAGLI ORTI / Getty Images)

Fig. 19: An eighth-century helm. (York Museums Trust, CC BY-SA 4.0)

Fig. 20: Photo taken on Rest Hill Road in front of the proposed battleground. (Michael Livingston)

Fig. 21: The topography of the northern end of the Wirral peninsula seen through Lidar imagery. (Michael Livingston)

Fig. 22: Old Bank today, at the confluence of the Fender and Birket. (Brian Griffiths)

Fig. 23: The area likely immediately behind Anlaf's lines in 937. (Pete Holder)

Fig. 24: Looking west towards the Dee. (Pete Holder)

Fig. 25: The view over the battlefield, looking north. (Pete Holder)

Fig. 26: The Clatterbrook today. (Brian Griffiths)

Fig. 27: Looking south down the zig-zagging line of the Clatterbrook. (Pete Holder)

Fig. 28: The battleground as the English may have seen it. (Dave Capener)

Fig. 29: A Scandinavian arrowhead recovered by Wirral Archaeology. (Paul Sherman)

Fig. 30: A badly corroded arrowhead recovered by Wirral Archaeology. (Paul Sherman)

Fig. 31: A strap end recovered by Wirral Archaeology. (Paul Sherman)

Fig. 32: Gaming pieces recovered by Wirral Archaeology. (Paul Sherman)

Fig. 33: An Athelstan penny. (York Museums Trust, CC BY-SA 4.0)

Fig. 34: An effigy of Athelstan. (Photo by Geography Photos/Universal Images Group via Getty Images)

List of Maps

The British Isles, *c.* 937

Sea, swamp or alluvium
Roman roads
Alfred/Guthrum Treaty line

ORKNEY ISLANDS

CAITHNESS

HEBRIDES

Moray Firth
• Inverness

MOUNTH   • Dunnottar

KINGDOM OF SCOTS

IONA

North Sea

Antonine Wall
Firth of Forth
Dumbarton   Edinburgh

DAL RIATA

Lindisfarne
• Bamburgh

KINGDOM OF STRATHCLYDE

Firth of Clyde

Hadrian's Wall
Corbridge   • Chester-le-street
• Carlisle
Solway Firth
• Eamont

NORTHUMBRIA

ISLE OF MAN

Skipton   York

IRELAND

Irish Sea

• Beverley

Humber

Brunanburh
⚔   Manchester
Chester   Lincoln
ANGLESEY   Nottingham
GWYNEDD   Derby
Wroxeter   Tamworth
POWYS

Wash

Clonmacnoise   Dublin

Limerick

Norwich

EAST ANGLIA

Stamford

MERCIA

WALES   • Worcester

DEHEUBARTH   • Hereford
Carmarthen •
GWENT   Cirencester

ESSEX   • Colchester

GLYWYSING
Bristol Channel   Malmesbury   Abingdon
WESSEX   London   *Thames*
THANET
Athelney •
Winchester SUSSEX   KENT
Canterbury •
Exeter •   Hastings
ISLE OF WIGHT

CORNWALL

English Channel

N

0   100 miles
0   100km

Introduction

A Field of Death, 937

It was early October. In other parts of Britain, on the farms that war had left abandoned, crops of late wheat stood ready for the scythe to cut them down. Here, at Brunanburh, the crop on the field had been men, and the harvest had been bountiful.

Most medieval battles ended quickly. As lines closed in upon one another, as the prospect of violent death grew nearer, even the bravest would find their courage wavering. If but a single man broke and ran, panic could spread through the line like fire racing through dry straw. Formations could collapse into rout. As they fled, most of those who died took it in the back.

Not here. Not this day.

At Brunanburh the preparations for battle had begun in the crisp air before the dawn, and the first light had glinted from ready, sharpened spears upon a still-green field. The blood-letting, once begun, wouldn't end until the last combatants fell upon a shoreline, miles away, as that same sun descended in the west.

In time Brunanburh would prove one of the most important battles in history. It's often been said that no day can better claim to have borne witness to the birth of England. More accurately said, it was the day that England grew up, in a bloody coming of age.

Battles are among the most dramatic moments in history. However fascinating the political manoeuvrings that lead up to them, the personal antagonisms behind them, or the careful campaigns that bring the players to the field, on the stage of battle all that remains is life and death, those who walk away and those who do not.

Hollywood reflects this dramatic truth, both with lingering shots of the tense quiet that proceeds the throaty roar, and long, drawn-out sequences of carnage and courage when the fighting begins. Rarely do the movies spend their time on the inglorious aftermath, the reality of the sights, sounds, and smells that the survivors experienced.

THE KING AND THE DEAD

If Athelstan, the victorious king of the English, stepped away from the revelries of the living and walked to the edge of the field, the fires of the encampment behind him would have stretched his shadow across ruts of torn earth and piles of broken bodies. But the camp light would not have reached far: the New Moon came on the 7th, so even a cloudless night would have lowered a deep shroud of darkness across most of the carnage on this early October night.

The sounds of his surviving men moving among the tents in camp would have faded in and out behind him, like the call of a nightingale passing between trees. Athelstan was 43 years old this day, and it's easy to imagine him with grey salting his beard and fatigue in his eyes. If a breeze came over the hillsides, stirring against the trampled blades of grass at his feet, it would have done little to disturb the shoulder-length drape of his hair, sweat-matted from his helm. The bridge of his nose was reddened, might well have been bruised, from the smashing of that same helmet's nasal guard against his skin. And despite the hard-won callouses of a lifetime around sword, spear, and shield, his hands would have ached from this long day's struggle.

Athelstan was by all accounts a devout man. So he surely prayed for the souls of the Christians among the dead. He might well have spared a thought for the pagans, too, of whom there were many. For the dead found worthy of salvation he probably gave orders for their transport to holy places, to be buried in sacred ground.

It could be, as we imagine the king looking out across the dark field, that the monks had already begun their long walks to begin this final, gruesome task. If so, the king may have heard the noise of the first wagons arriving.

Regardless, it is certain that, as he looked out over the devastation, this man for whom it all had happened – for or against his rule, there was no cause else – would have seen flickering pools of feeble light floating through the inky blackness: torches in the hands of people combing the fields. Some of these were no doubt seeking friends or brothers, here and there pulling living men out from beneath the cold weight of the fallen. Given the vastness of the destruction and the piling of corpses at the lines of engagement, such horrors would have been inevitable. They were rarely recorded, though – no doubt for the same reason that our movies rarely provide more than a passing glance at these lingering aftermaths: no one wishes to dwell on these images. In fact, one of our only acknowledgments of such bitter realities in the Middle Ages comes from the battle of Crécy in 1346, when a poet-herald who had been in the fight regretted that the more knowledgeable of the other heralds could not help identify the French dead. His name was Colins of Beaumont, and after the fight he wrote of these still living men:

Guillaume, however, was discovered
Among the dead, wounded in the face and body,
The night after the battle,
And then indeed Huet Cholet, without doubt,
Was found on the third day after the battle,
Which was certainly directly confirmed.
Let Honour have them, I insist,
Ranged with the dead in her records,
For they had been left for dead.[1]

There were other realities of the aftermath that were rarely recorded, and they, too, would have been among the pools of torchlight Athelstan could have seen moving over the field. The dead held value in their armour, their weapons, their purses full of coins, the rings upon their fingers, and even the blood-sodden clothes they wore. The margins of the Bayeux Tapestry, which famously illustrates the battle of Hastings in 1066, show this happening even in the climactic moment of the death of King Harold II Godwinson. As Harold is being struck down by a man on horseback, the margin below shows opportunistic survivors stripping the dead of everything they can. Shirts of mail are drawn off corpses. A man gathers swords. Two others appear to squabble over a shield.

Some of those stripping the dead at Brunanburh might even have been their fellow fighters, the survivors who viewed such materials as part of their reward for survival. Others were searching for the choicest prizes, the riches of fallen princes, which were being gathered in the name of the victorious king. This may be what the man gathering swords in the Bayeux Tapestry was doing. Still others, though, perhaps skulking through the destruction without light, were war-followers, who had accompanied the armies or tracked them for the chance to pick over the leavings.

Athelstan surely would have thought of the last of these scavenging groups as thieves – no different than the birds and the beasts who had already descended on the field to feast upon the bountiful harvest that war provided.

It was this dark feast that sat in the memory of an unnamed poet who wrote the poem now known as *The Battle of Brunanburh*. The work survives in several manuscripts of the *Anglo-Saxon Chronicle*, the sole information it gives for the year 937.[2] Scholars debate when the poem was composed – whether shortly after the battle or a few years later under the reign of Athelstan's brother and heir, Edmund. For our purposes, it may be the closest thing that exists to a contemporary account of what happened. It is, without question, the single most important source we have for the battle, and we will call on it more than once over the course of this book. Here's how its poet describes the aftermath of the victory won by the English:

They left behind to divide the corpses
the dark-coated one, the black raven,
the horn-beaked one, and the dusk-coated one:

the white-tailed eagle, to enjoy the carrion,
that greedy war-hawk, and that grey beast,
the wolf of the wood. Never greater slaughter
was there on this island, never as many
folk felled before this
by the swords' edges, as those books tell us,
old authorities, since here from the east
the Angles and Saxons came ashore.[3]

We cannot know how many men had died. Five young kings had fallen, the same poet informs us, and seven earls from across the sea, but the rest were simply 'countless'[4] – a measure, no doubt, of both their immense number and the little regard their leaders had for tracking individual deaths beyond the ranks of their own leadership and kin. 'Never greater slaughter', as he says. The birds and the beasts would have had their fill.

Legend says that the feeding of ravens was also on the mind of another poet on the field this night. According to the saga that now bears his name, Egil Skallagrimson was among the men searching for familiar faces among the dead. *Egil's Saga* is likely the work of an Icelandic politician and writer named Snorri Sturluson (1179–1241), to whose hand we owe many of our most important written sources on the history and culture of the Northern European (Norse) peoples that we often call the Vikings. Whether from Snorri's hand or not – though I'll write here under the assumption that it is – the saga seems to come from his time period: roughly three centuries after the battle. This alone may give reason to doubt its accuracy. But Snorri appears to have been a careful writer who made considerable use of traditional materials that had been handed down through generations of a culture that kept stories, sayings, and even laws via oral tradition. Among these earlier materials quoted by Snorri are snippets of poetry said to have been composed by Egil himself.

The Norse sagas are full of fascinating characters, but few can hold a candle to Egil Skallagrimson. Born on an Icelandic farmstead, Egil wrote his first poem at the age of three, used an axe to split the skull of another boy at the age of seven, and headed to Latvia for his first round of plundering at the age of twelve. Eventually, beside his loyal brother Thorolf, he became one of the most feared outlaws, mighty warriors, and renowned poets in the Viking world. By the time of Brunanburh, the twisting road of his life had brought him and Thorolf into the pay of King Athelstan. Egil was in his early 30s, and the saga describes him as being a fearsome and unusual sight:

> Egil had very distinctive features, with a wide forehead, bushy brows, and a nose that was not long but extremely broad. His upper jaw was broad and long, and his chin and jawbones were exceptionally wide. With his thick neck and stout shoulders, he stood out from other men. When he was angry, his face grew harsh and fierce. He was well built and taller than other men, with thick wolf-grey hair, although he had gone bald at an early age.[5]

It may be that this extraordinary set of features is artistic hyperbole, but beginning in 1984 with the work of Thordur Hardarson, scholars began to ponder whether they were indicative of Paget's Disease, which causes misshapen, often abnormally large bones – especially in the skull. Whether or not this is so – I personally don't think it is – we can be sure that Egil would have been a striking figure even among the most battle-scarred men upon the field of Brunanburh.

In fact, *Egil's Saga* claims Egil stood out not just in appearance but in leadership. Among the thousands of men who defended the English against the Vikings this bloody day, Snorri tells us that Egil and his brother Thorolf were in the forefront: Vikings standing against Vikings.

After the battle, the saga says, Egil chased the fleeing remnants of the enemy all the way to the distant shore of the sea. He slew an enemy earl that the saga names as Adils. Then he returned to the main battlefield to find the body of his fallen brother among the strewn dead.

Egil and his men washed and dressed Thorolf's corpse. They dug for him a grave. Egil himself removed two of his own golden arm-rings – torque-styled bracelets – and placed them on his brother's arms. And then, as he and his men piled rocks and earth over the grave to form a burial mound, Egil composed a poem.

VIKING POETRY

Poetry had a special place in the hearts of the Norse (an umbrella term for both the Scandinavians and Vikings). Like the myth of Prometheus, the Greek god who had stolen fire from the gods to warm men's hearths, the Norse told stories of how Odin had stolen the gift of poetry from rival gods to warm their hearts.[6]

Such was the power of poetry that it was not uncommon for Scandinavian armies, in the moments before battle, to send forth rival poets to engage in verbal combats called *flytings*. In practice, these were rather like rap battles: an elaborate jousting of taunts and braggadocio. Indeed, the word *brag* in English has connections to Bragi, the Norse god of poetry and music who welcomed slain warriors into the halls of Valhalla.

Because medieval poetry will appear more than once in this book – and because it can be very different from the poetry we are used to reading today – it is useful to take a very brief look at how it works. As it happens, Egil's poem at the grave of his brother Thorolf is a textbook example of Norse poetry in particular. Here's how Snorri records it in the original language:

Gekk, sás óðisk ekki,
jarlmanns bani snarla,
þreklundaðr fell, Þundar,
Þórólfr, í gný stórum.
Jörð grær, en vér verðum,
Vínu nær of mínum,
helnauð es þat, hylja
harm, ágætum barma.[7]

Rather than end-rhymes, this poem is dependent on rhythms of emphasis and internal rhymes, which can be marked out across the first two lines by bold type and underlines, respectively:

> **Gekk**, sás óðisk <u>ek</u>ki,
> <u>jarl</u>manns **bani** <u>snarl</u>a,

Such intricate structuring meant that poets very often had to play with word order in order to fit sounds into their appropriate spaces. The first four lines of the poem, for instance, would be word-for-word translated something like this:

> Strode, nothing fearing,
> belonging-to-the-earl of-death snare,
> bold-hearted fell, of-the-Thunder-god,
> Thorolf, into the din.

For many of us today, the effect of this confused syntax is bewilderment. For the Norse listener, however, it provoked a sense of wonder and interest as the listeners worked to fit the pieces into meaning. Intricacy and difficulty was one of its finer traits.

Here's a more readable translation of the whole of Egil's poem:

> The earl's death-snare,
> nothing fearing, strode forth
> into the Thunder-god's din:
> bold-hearted, Thorolf fell.
> Earth grows, travels over him,
> close beside *Vínu*.[8]
> My despair is the same, as I hide
> my sorrow, glorious brother.

Even presenting this in a traditional word order still leaves more to do. Another part of the work of understanding this kind of poetry involves decoding compact metaphors called kennings: often two nouns fused together in order to refer to a third. Here, as an example, a 'snare' is a trap, so the 'death-snare' of the earl is the man who killed him, Thorolf. On top of all this, Egil uses the external imagery of his brother's burial to produce a powerful reflection of his own internal sorrows: just as the earth covers Thorolf's dead body, so must Egil cover over his despair at his brother's loss.

Strange as it may seem, a measure of poetic excellence among the Norse was just how much *work* all this decipherment took: the decoding of metaphors, the surprising twists of references, and the puzzling complexities made for great entertainment.

After reciting these lines, *Egil's Saga* says, the warrior composed yet another verse. This time, beyond his personal loss, he spoke of his deeds and of the deaths of his enemies, who were led by a man we will meet later, named Anlaf:

> I cast up corpse-mounds, west
> of the field before the battle-flags.
> Fierce was the storm when I struck
> Adils with the blue Adder.
> Young Anlaf with the Angles
> made a thunder of steel.
> The ravens had no hunger,
> when Hring came to the weapon-assembly.[9]

With that, Egil left the mounds of earth, the corpses, and the ravens, and sought out the king for whom so many had fought and died.

GIFTS OF THE KING

We simply can't know whether the scene that unfolds in *Egil's Saga* is at all accurate. The story of Egil is undoubtedly embellished in details large and small, but in respect to what follows it certainly has the ring of truth: if what the saga describes didn't happen to Egil, something like it probably happened to someone *like* Egil.

By the time Egil found him, the saga says, the king had ridden to a fortress south of the battlefield.

The hall had a central fire lit against the October cold, though few would have heard the popping, crackling logs amid the raucous revelry of the men. On one side of the warming flames were long wooden tables, benches filled with English warriors and their allies. On the other side, at the head of the hall, was the raised dais where Athelstan himself sat at the high bench, aglow with firelight and winning glory. The alcohol was flowing freely – both to help embrace survival and to forget the day's horrors – and the voices raised in song or boast or laughter were loud.

Egil had helped bring the king victory, but the loss of his brother cut him deeply. He was in a dark mood when he entered the noisy hall. Athelstan, seeing the large man enter, ordered that a bench be cleared in one of the foremost places of honour, directly before the king's seat on the other side of the hearth. Still fully armed and armoured – no doubt still streaked with the gore of battle – Egil took the offered seat, dropping his shield at his feet. But he didn't remove his helm. Nor did he drink when a horn sloshing with mead was brought to him. Instead, the brows above his glaring eyes lowering with menace, the Viking made a show of placing his sheathed sword across his knees. As he stared at the king, he pulled it half out of its scabbard before slamming it back home – again and again.

Whatever the cultural and linguistic differences between the English and the Viking warrior might have been, there was no misreading Egil's gesture. He and his brother had shed blood for the king. As the saga presents it, Athelstan's tactical decisions on the field had a direct role in causing Thorolf's death.

Your move, king.

Athelstan had his own sword upon his knees, and for minutes the two men stared at each other across the dancing flames.

The hall grew tense. Egil's provocation was there for all to see. The empty cups pounding against the benches went silent. Everyone waited for the king to respond.

At last, Athelstan drew his blade, baring the steel to the light of the dancing flames. Still seated, he removed one of his own golden arm-rings.

Had he noticed that Egil's were now gone? Had he somehow received word that they were buried now with his brother?

The king slipped the ring over the point of his sword, stood, and stepped down onto the floor. He walked to the edge of the fire, across from the hulking warrior. Then he stretched out his arm, extending the blade and the hanging ring over the flames.

Egil stood and strode to the fire, opposite the king. He unsheathed his own sword completely now. Reaching out, he put the tip of it through the offered arm-ring and took it. The two men withdrew to their seats. Egil, sitting down, fitted the ring to his arm. He unclasped his helmet and his armour. His face relaxed. A drinking horn that he'd refused was close at hand, and he picked it up and drank it down to the bottom. Then, at last, he spoke in verse:

> The lord of the mail-coat lets hang
> a metal bracelet on my arm,
> upon my hawk-trodden wrist,
> that perch of hunting-birds.
> I brandish it on the breaker of shields,
> the arm that feeds ravens.
> That sword-gallows brings,
> in the spear-storm, greater glory.[10]

The tension broke. Athelstan had defused the situation. The symbolism of the king's own arm-ring clasped about the warrior's right arm – the one that would have swung the shield-shattering, raven-feeding sword – could not be mistaken: the king respected this warrior. Nor could the symbolism of its transfer through fire be forgotten: Egil and his brother had indeed passed through fire, and the flames of war had taken Thorolf's life. Egil's poem showed that he accepted this public display of gratitude, but it also, far more subtly, showed that his pain of loss was still real. The phrase 'lord of the mail-coat' is in Snorri's original language 'brynju Höðr' – literally the Höðr of the byrnie (a coat of mail-armour). Höðr, in Norse religion, was a blind son of Odin, tricked by Loki into slaying his own brother and fellow god, Baldr. His name was synonymous with 'war', which in its chaos slaughters with blind fury. An arm-ring, no matter its golden shine, could not erase the darkness of Thorolf's death.

The revelry within the hall returned – all the noisier now for the addition of Egil and any of the men who might have accompanied him. After a time, Athelstan directed that two chests be brought in, so heavy that it took two men to carry each of them. Both were full of silver. It was a breath-taking sight. More wealth than most men would see in their lifetimes. The king offered them both to Egil, to take back to Iceland and give to his father and his kinsmen there in recompense for the death of Thorolf. He gave Egil his friendship, and offered him land and title should he wish to stay in his kingdom. Not surprisingly, *Egil's Saga* has the warrior reply in verse:

> For pain the jutting peaks
> over my eyes knew how to droop.
> Now have I found one who flattened
> the furrows on my forehead.
> The king has pushed the crags
> from the ground of my face,
> the fences from my eyes:
> he is unbending in bracelets.[11]

Egil would remain in the kingdom through the winter. It was probably sometime over those next months that he composed a poem in honour of King Athelstan that reflected on what had been won at Brunanburh. Snorri gives us only a single verse of it, along with its refrain:

> Now has the earth-shield,
> the battle messenger,
> three earls felled,
> all fallen under the kin of Ella.
> Athelstan achieved more,
> the kin-famous king conquers all,
> this I swear, to the breaker
> of the wave of fire, king of men.[12]

Three enemy leaders slain, he says, by the kin of Ella: a reference
to a Northumbrian king who, according to the Norse sagas, had
been responsible for the defeat and execution of the legendary
Norse warrior, Ragnar Lodbrok – by throwing him into a pit
of venomous snakes. In vengeance of this, in 866 Ragnar's sons
led what is generally called the Great Heathen Army to attack
Northumbria. They had killed Ella, seized York, and begun the
cycle of war between the English and Vikings that had now
ended – so it was believed that winter in 937 – on the field of
Brunanburh. For in the aftermath of that victory, the idea of an
England that we would recognize today was at last realized: from
Cornwall to Kent, and spreading north to Hadrian's Wall and
perhaps – as the refrain of Egil's poem for Athelstan says – even to
the highlands far beyond:

> Now lie the high reindeer hills
> under Athelstan's rule.[13]

Whatever the full truth of Egil's story – we will return to it – we can
be sure of the field of death, the mourning for the fallen, the relief
of the survivors, and the awarding of prizes and compensation.
Whether the warrior-poet was there or not, these things stand.

We can be sure, too, that as the sun came up over the battlefield
the next morning, the business of stripping the dead was in full
swing. The new day brought surety to the English that their
defeated enemies were not coming back. It also brought clarity to
the scale of the destruction.

Many of the corpse-robbers who had held sway through the
night – man, bird, and beast – had faded back into the shadows of
the surrounding forests. In their place were those men who were
formally tasked with systematically transferring dead men's wealth
to living men's pockets.

This formal battle recycling would have been common and
expected, though it is little described. Like the fields of the
dead themselves, this scene is not one that most people want to
remember. But there are glimpses, as in this account from a citizen

of Valenciennes about the actions taken by the victorious English after the battle of Crécy:

> And at the end of two days [after the battle] the English had taken so much armour from the dead, so that seemed good to them, the king put all the remaining armour, used and new, good and bad, in a large place amid the field, and burned them all, so that no one could ever use them again.[14]

The gathering and sorting of these materials was gruesome and unceremonious work. Nothing came clean from the battle, but the sooner it was recycled the sooner the carnage could be left behind. Blacksmiths, armourers, and other craftsmen who before the battle had worked on field forges to repair weapons, armours, wagons, and so much else that was needed for an army on the move now found themselves pressed into service salvaging what they could as quickly as they could. Corpses were searched and stripped, their belongings gathered and brought to sorting sites where what was intact and useful was separated from what could be melted down and recycled for its valuable metals. Leather straps were cut to get gear off bodies. Frozen buckles were pried apart. Useable spearheads were pulled off snapped shafts, and those that couldn't be reused were thrown into a pile for melting down in the fires that were stoked as hot as the men could manage.

And here and there, under their feet, the detritus of war was pressed into the mud, forgotten in the haste to just be done. Spearheads went into the ground. Shattered buckles. Even broken swords. Such was the scale of Brunanburh that thousands of these bits and pieces of the battle could have been pushed into the bloodied earth before and after this moment and no one would have batted an eye.

In a short time, perhaps only days, Athelstan's men had departed. Some returned to their farms and families. Others were laid to rest in graves. Some others went to the scavenging beasts.

Only the metal remained. Rusting beneath the earth.

For over a thousand years. Silent as ghosts.

The Birth of England, to 865

Most schoolchildren are taught that England owes its name to the Angles, one of several tribes that migrated to the British Isles during the era of Roman withdrawal around the fifth century: England is Angle-land. What precipitated these movements – which traditionally have been called the Anglo-Saxon Invasions on account of two of the biggest such tribes – isn't known, but the story is usually told something like this: waves of Germanic-speaking peoples struck the shores of Britain. In fits and starts, the existing population of Britons was rolled back ahead of this rising tide or subsumed by it. New cultural orders were forged, coalescing over the next centuries into something we could call England.

Of course, what it means to be English today doesn't rest on one's Angle-ness. Nevertheless, from a historical standpoint of understanding how the nation of England was born – and thus how it came of age at Brunanburh – it will be useful to look at what is actually known about these invasions, including whether they really happened at all.

This means a trip into the so-called Dark Ages.

THE DARK AGES

A remarkable, but largely forgotten monument of the Dark Ages stands today in a quiet Welsh valley: a broken pillar of stone, placed atop a grass-covered ancient barrow. Every day cars pass by, as tourists come to take photos of the haunting ruins of a 13th-century abbey just along the road, one of the most picturesque in Britain. Few take note of this lonely assemblage of rock off the side of the road, a monument that was first raised upon the existing Bronze Age barrow in the middle of the ninth century and thenceforth gave the place its name: Valle Crucis, the valley of the cross.

For the rare visitors who *do* stop to look upon the monument, a short fence raised around it keeps them from getting too close. Nearby, the government has placed a small, informational sign that identifies it as the Pillar of Eliseg: time and the predations of men have stripped from it the form of the cross and left behind only its upright shaft, but it nevertheless remains a remarkable sight.

There is no fee to approach the fence. No guard stands watch. No visitor centre exists to give proper credit to the fact that this deceptively simple finger of rock is an important source in our efforts to unlock the secrets of a period often called Britain's Dark Ages.

The Dark Ages – with the exception of a short but horrifying time around 536 in which Britain likely experienced a 'year without a summer' (probably due to volcanic activity elsewhere in the world)[1] – are not called 'dark' because they lacked physical sunlight. Nor, despite what Hollywood likes to portray, are they 'dark' because they lacked moral or social civility. To the contrary, the Dark Ages are 'dark' because we know so little about them: the darkness upon the age is the shadow of *our* ignorance, not theirs.

Many historians nevertheless reject the term Dark Ages, arguing that it is often very inappropriately equated with the *whole* of the Middle Ages – a historical period with its own definitional problems, but one I have elsewhere defined as falling roughly between the battle of Adrianople in 378 and the second siege of Rhodes in 1522.[2] I'm certainly no fan of calling the Middle Ages as a whole the Dark Ages: we know a great deal about a great many parts of this period, and it was often a lively and absolutely vibrant time.

But it is equally true and important to admit that there are gaps in our knowledge. Shadows fall here and there across the whole range of the Middle Ages, sometimes small, sometimes big. It is useful to observe this. And it is particularly useful to point out that perhaps no shadow is bigger, no darkness deeper, than the one that falls on Britain in particular from the fourth to the sixth century. These years, which witnessed the retreat of Rome, are the Dark Ages of Britain's history. It's a time for which there are far too few sources to shed light on what was happening and when.

Few surviving sources, anyway. It's essential to observe, after all, that the Dark Ages weren't so dark to the people who lived within them. They knew what was happening around them and why it was happening – at least as much as *anyone* ever understands such things about their world. And they undoubtedly communicated their knowledge to one another. The period must have been abundant with rich oral tradition, and for all we know it might have been rich with different kinds of written materials, too. If it was, though, little of these materials have survived. Time is an unrelenting and unforgiving eraser of the works of men.

Though it was made of stone, time didn't spare the Pillar of Eliseg. The text chiselled into it is difficult to read now. Some of the old stone is missing, and years of exposure to the weather have taken their toll upon what is left. Fortunately for us, the monument is no modern discovery. A Welsh scholar named Edward Lhuyd, who was then keeper of the Ashmolean Museum, passed through Valle Crucis on a research trip in 1696. Along the way he dutifully copied down the inscription as he could then read it. What he found carved into the rock was already fragmentary, but he managed to record 31 lines of a Latin text. The fact that these lines are, altogether, one of the longest surviving inscriptions from pre-Viking Wales, serves as a reminder of how rare such sources are, and how precious. The Pillar reads:

† Cyngen son of Cattell, son of Brochfael, son of Elisedd, son of Gwylog:
† This Cyngen, the great-grandson of Elisedd, erected this stone for his great-grandfather Elisedd.
† This same Elisedd united the kingdom of Powys ... moreover through force ... from the control of the Angles ... his gains with sword and with fire.

† Whosoever shall recite this hand-carved ... let him give a blessing upon the soul of Eliseg.

† This same Cyngen ... hand ... to his own kingdom of Powys ... and which ... the mountain ... monarchy ... Maximus of Britain ... Pascent ... Maun Annan ... Britu, moreover, was blessed by Germanus and was the son of Vortigern and Severa, the daughter of King Maximus, who killed the king of the Romans.

† Conmarch created this writing at the behest of his king, Cyngen.

† The blessing of the Lord upon Cyngen and also upon all his family and all the kingdom of Powys until ...

We don't know all of these individuals. What we think we know of some doesn't necessarily fit with what the inscription says about their genealogy or background. Still, the Pillar of Eliseg is massively useful, beginning with the fact that it mentions both Vortigern, who holds a central place in the history of Dark Age Britain, and Maximus, a Roman who might well have begun the Dark Ages in the first place.

ROMAN AND POST-ROMAN BRITAIN

Around 325 BC, the Greek explorer Pytheas of Massalia sailed around the British Isles. Though his own account of the voyage does not survive, secondary records of it do. They report that the islands were called by him Bretannikē, after the Celtic-speaking tribes who lived there, and the name stuck. The native tribes encountered by Pytheas and subsequent visitors were hardly a unified group, but they had enough in common that historians generally speak of the Britons to refer to them as a whole, while nevertheless recognizing that their histories are far foggier than we would like: a Dark Ages before the Dark Ages, in a way.

Julius Caesar twice attempted to invade the island of Great Britain in 55 and 54 BC, but permanent Roman conquest didn't start until the reign of Claudius in AD 43. The Romans extended their control north to the vicinity of the stone Hadrian's Wall in 122, then even further to the turf-and-wood Antonine Wall in 142 – though how much the walls mark the border between lands under imperial control and those that were not remains an open question. Regardless, over time the Britons and the Romans intermingled such that historians usually talk of a Romano-British population occupying much of Great Britain.

It's often said that the Romans left Britain in the year 410. This was the year of the so-called Rescript of Honorius, in which the Western Roman emperor Honorius (r. 393–423) wrote to the people of the cities of Britain that he was not in a position to provide them with military aid. These letters from Honorius don't survive, but their existence is claimed in the work of Zosimus, who was writing in distant Constantinople at the end of the century.[3] Though a few historians have tried to attack the reliability of Zosimus' account here – he's painfully wrong on more than a few matters – no convincing case has been made that he's incorrect about the existence of these letters specifically. At the very least, the letters would fit into a wider context of imperial difficulties that culminated, on 24 August of that year, with the sack of Rome by Visigoths under the control of Alaric.[4]

Assuming they were real, it's doubtful that the emperor would write the letters to the Romano-British for no reason. That is, he would surely be responding, in the negative, to a request for aid. But aid against whom?

Another fifth-century work, the *Gallic Chronicle of A.D. 452*, informs us that in late 408 or 409 'Saxon' invaders – this could be any of a number of Germanic tribes – had struck and devastated Britain. Once again, Zosimus might be able to fill in some of the story if we dare trust him on the point[5]: by the end of 409 the Britons had beaten back the invaders, but in the process they had also expelled the Roman officials and established their own government. In other words, when imperial Roman strength failed to stop the Saxons, the Romano-Britons apparently revolted against imperial rule and barbarian invasion both. It might have been these expelled imperialists who wrote to Honorius for help, and the emperor, already in a hard bind, said they were on their own. The scope of the Roman administrative loss in Britain might be seen in the emperor's choice of addressee for his letters: he wrote to the people of the formerly Roman cities, because there was no longer a working imperial administration with which he could communicate.

So perhaps the revolt against Roman rule in 409 would be a better date for the end of Roman Britain than the Roman refusal to send help in 410. On the other hand, we have little idea of the process, timing, and impact of the Roman departure across the whole of Great Britain. It's doubtful that it was all at once, and the 'revolt', insofar as we might imagine it from the sparse bits of information that are left to us, might have been a leadership struggle that nevertheless left the mechanisms of governance for the daily lives of the population relatively unchanged.[6] Archaeological remains from the period certainly don't show signs of a great calamity. So exactly when the Romans might be said to have retreated probably depends, when all is said and done, on what we mean when we talk about the retreat of Rome.

For a British monk named Gildas, writing a sermon sometime in the sixth century, there seems little doubt at all that it was the departure of the Roman legions that mattered, and he was certain he knew the date and the man responsible for it.

THE SCATHING SERMON

According to a ninth-century biography written about him – he had, by this point, become *Saint* Gildas – Gildas was born into a wealthy Romano-British family that ruled territory somewhere between the Antonine Wall and Hadrian's Wall.

Gildas' older brother became king after their father's death. As younger brothers often did in those days, Gildas became a monk. He studied first at a monastery in the modern Welsh town of Llantwit Major, after which his travels took him to Ireland, Rome, and Ravenna before he eventually founded a monastery of his own across the English Channel in Brittany, where he died.

It was while he was living in Brittany that Gildas wrote the work for which he is now known: a sermon entitled *De Excidio et Conquestu Britanniae* (On the Ruin and Conquest of Britain).

Not surprisingly, *The Ruin of Britain*, as I will abbreviate its title, is an angry work. Gildas makes no effort to hide his absolute horror at what became of his homeland and its native people after the year 383. It was in that year that Magnus Maximus, a leader of Roman military forces in Britain, took many (most?) of the imperial legions across the English Channel in order to support his claim to be emperor on the Continent. As Gildas puts it:

> Britain was despoiled of her whole army, her military resources, her governors, brutal as they were, and her sturdy youth, who had followed in the tyrant's [i.e. Maximus'] footsteps, never to return home. Quite ignorant of the ways of war, she groaned aghast for many years, trodden under foot first by two exceedingly savage overseas nations, the Scots from the north-west and the Picts from the north.[7]

So, some years after 383, other native groups within the British Isles began attacking the Romano-Britons: the Scots (from Ireland) and the Picts (from Scotland). As their northern borders collapsed under this pressure, Gildas claims that foolish Romano-Briton leaders – led by Vortigern, named on the Pillar of Eliseg – eventually invited foreign Saxons into their lands to serve as mercenaries who might help them fight back.

> Then all the members of the council, together with that proud tyrant [i.e., Vortigern], were struck blind; the guard – or rather the method of destruction – they devised for our land was that the ferocious Saxons (name not to be spoken!), hated by man and God, should be let into the island like wolves into the fold, to beat back the peoples of the north. Nothing more destructive, nothing more bitter has ever befallen the land. How utter the blindness of their minds! How desperate and crass the stupidity![8]

Nothing of Vortigern's plans would have been terribly surprising in Roman terms. By this time the Empire had a long record of using auxiliary forces in order to further its aims. Unfortunately, as Gildas' imagery implies, the invited Saxons turned against their hosts, and, as Gildas laments,

> In just punishment for the crimes that had gone before, a fire heaped up and nurtured by the hand of the impious easterners spread from sea to sea. It devastated town and country round about, and, once it was alight, it did not die down until it had burned almost the whole surface of the island and was licking the western ocean with its fierce red tongue.[9]

No one writes truly unbiased history, but some histories are very much more biased than others. Gildas' sermon wasn't intended as history in the way that we now understand the word. His biases are clear and deep running. This is nevertheless one of our best contemporary sources for political and cultural information about what was happening in this part of the Dark Ages ... which makes it enormously frustrating that there are so many gaps in what he's telling us. Perhaps none of these gaps is bigger than exactly *when* these Saxons arrived – since this Saxon invasion does not appear to be the same one described by the *Gallic Chronicle of AD 452* as taking place in 408 or 409: the Saxons were defeated in that earlier war, but in this one they were victorious.

Gildas tries. He states that he himself was born in 'the year of the siege of Badon Hill', an apparently major engagement in which the native Britons were (momentarily) victorious over the invaders. This same year, he writes, was 44 years before his writing.[10] Gildas has thereby provided multiple triangulated events – his birth, his writing, Badon Hill, and this massive Saxon arrival – such that knowing any date will lead to the rest. But he doesn't provide even one.

Among our many challenges in history is the fact that the further we push back in time from the present, the greater the problems we face in dating events. The sources for such an early period as this rarely, if ever, provide the kind of chronological accounting of dates that we would like. This reality can be deeply frustrating, but it's also inevitable: the sources don't give clear dates on a timeline because they often don't *have* a timeline.

Our modern lives are so bound by calendars and a sequencing of time widely utilized throughout the world that it's hard to imagine a reality without such things as we understand them. Yet the fact is that even time – or at least our reckoning of it – had a beginning. The calendar we are accustomed to using – according to which it is 2020 at time of writing – is called the Anno Domini system of dating, and it was invented by a Christian monk named Dionysius Exiguus around the year 525. Prior to this system, numerous dating methods were used, almost all of them dependent, to one degree or another, on relative dating procedures. A popular Roman method, for instance, had been to date an event by who held the consulship in that year: thus Dionysius dates his work establishing the Anno Domini system by saying it occurred during the consulship of Probus Junior – which is not terribly useful without a knowledge of when that consulship occurred. Anno Domini dating instead established a sequential count of years. Needing a beginning point to start the count, the monk chose what he believed to be the year of the birth of Jesus of Nazareth – Anno Domini means 'Year of the Lord' in Latin – which he reckoned (incorrectly, scholars think) was 525 years before Probus Junior became consul. Gildas, writing before Anno Domini dating was popularized, provides such dates as he can, but 15 centuries later they are problematic.

Other sources provide more pieces to the puzzle, though never enough. Just to get the flavour of the problems, we can observe how Gildas' Vortigern was, according to the Pillar of Eliseg, the son-in-law of 'King Maximus'. Assuming he was of marrying age before Magnus Maximus departed in 383, Vortigern must have been born no later than the mid-360s. The *Anglo-Saxon Chronicle*, however, names Vortigern as commanding Romano-British forces against the invaders in 455 – at which point he would be roughly 90 years old! Is one of our sources in error? Are there two leaders named Vortigern? Is King Maximus not Magnus Maximus but instead Maximus of Hispania (r. 409–17), whose usurpation was strong enough for him to mint coins in his own name on the Iberian peninsula? That *might* work, except Maximus of Hispania isn't known to have ever come to Britain. So we would have to imagine some kind of implausible agreement at a distance in which he agreed to send a daughter overseas to marry Vortigern as part of an alliance for which there is *no* record at all. Worse, when the Romano-British leader needed aid to defend against the incursions of Picts and Scots, he didn't call on military help from Iberia but instead asked for mercenary help from the Saxons.

Things get far too speculative far too fast.

Trying to make sense of the Dark Ages is like spending five minutes in a room with the lights out and the shades drawn. You move around in the dark, stumbling into the furniture, feeling your way as best you can and listening to the clatter of things as you jar them about. Then, when you step out, someone gives you a piece of paper and asks you for a sketch of what was in there.

Again, the Dark Ages aren't 'dark' because of anything *wrong* with them. If we could go back, turn on the lights and throw open the shutters, we would see the inside of that room, in all its detail. It would be as clear to us as our own hands. The darkness is our own disappointing ignorance.

When it comes to the Dark Ages of Britain, then, about the only thing we can really say for certain is that one way or another, at one time or another, Rome departed. Sometime after that, Germanic tribes of Angles, Saxons, Jutes, and more came to Great Britain. If it was a migration in great force it left surprisingly little record on the landscape or in the remains left to us. Just as easily it could have been part of a steady, non-antagonistic stream of migration of peoples moving around the North Sea – into and out of Britain – that had been going on for centuries. Regardless, as Imperial Roman control loosened, there were sporadic struggles between the Romano-Britons and the Germanic tribes. It was hardly the kind of devastation that Gildas describes, but it was enough to begin tilting the dynamics of power. The Romano-Britons had some early victories. They fought the Saxons back in 409, if the *Gallic Chronicle* is accurate. The siege of Badon Hill was a win, whenever and whatever the hell it was. But power eventually slipped into the hands of those who would be associated – even if it was only in language – with the Germanic tribes.

That moment – if something so utterly vague can be called a moment – was the birth of England.

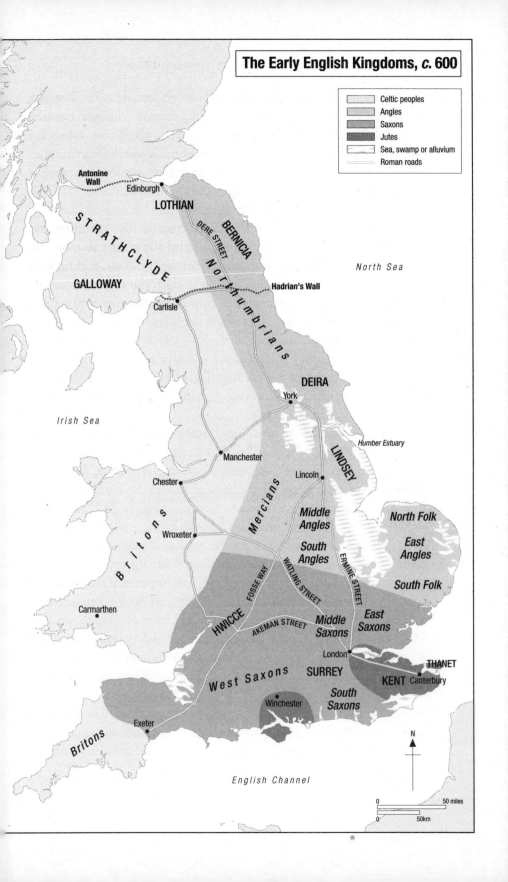

The Early English Kingdoms, *c.* 600

Legend:
- Celtic peoples
- Angles
- Saxons
- Jutes
- Sea, swamp or alluvium
- Roman roads

North Sea

Irish Sea

English Channel

Antonine Wall
Edinburgh
LOTHIAN
DERE STREET
BERNICIA
Northumbrians
STRATHCLYDE
GALLOWAY
Carlisle
Hadrian's Wall
DEIRA
York
Humber Estuary
LINDSEY
Manchester
Lincoln
Chester
Mercians
Middle Angles
North Folk
Britons
Wroxeter
South Angles
East Angles
FOSSE WAY
WATLING STREET
ERMINE STREET
South Folk
Carmarthen
HWICCE
AKEMAN STREET
Middle Saxons
East Saxons
East Saxons
London
THANET
West Saxons
SURREY
KENT Canterbury
Winchester
South Saxons
Exeter
Britons

N

0   50 miles
0   50km

Of course, none of these various cultural groups – the Britons, the Romans, the Angles, the Irish, the Vikings – should be seen through the lens of modern nationalism, which is a political concept essentially foreign to this period in Europe. What they had was something akin to what might be called patriotism today: a love of one's homeland. In the Carmarthen Museum, for instance, there stands the sixth-century tombstone of a man named Paulinus, which was discovered on a nearby farmstead. The inscription on it describes Paulinus as a lover of his country (*patriae amator*). It's impossible for us to say how he conceived of his *patria*, his country, but his love for it was real enough for him to be remembered for it. More than that, it was a love that others could understand: the message upon his tombstone was for the community of the living, after all, not the individual dead.

By the sixth century what we now think of as England was made up of seven kingdoms, now called the Heptarchy. Three of these kingdoms were identified with the Saxons: Essex (home of the East Saxons), Sussex (South Saxons), and Wessex (West Saxons). Three kingdoms were likewise associated with the Angles: East Anglia (whose division of North Folk and South Folk still lingers in the names Norfolk and Suffolk), Mercia, and Northumbria. A seventh kingdom, Kent, became the traditional home of the Jutes.

Roughly speaking, the power balance within the Heptarchy shifted by the century: Kent was the dominant kingdom in the sixth century, Northumbria in the seventh, and Mercia in the eighth (during which the Mercian king Offa built his 150-mile-long dyke to mark and defend the border between his kingdom and the Briton-controlled lands of Wales). The ninth century saw the rise of Wessex, due in no small part to the arrival, in 865, of what the *Anglo-Saxon Chronicle* calls the Great Heathen Army, but what I'll be calling the Great Viking Army. The kingdoms had seen Viking raids before, but this was recognizably different: an invasion force from across the sea, meant to stay.

Exactly where the Great Viking Army came from, who stood at its head, and how it led to the battle of Brunanburh, takes us across another sea – to Ireland.

The Vikings Arrive, 837–66

A century before the battle of Brunanburh, a Viking stood beside a dark-watered tidal pool. He'd come to Ireland on a longship, and that sleek-hulled craft had been drawn halfway up onto the shore behind him. Its sail was furled – rolled up against the crossbeam atop the ship's mast. Other men had stored their oars and pulled free the shields that had lined its long, low sides, which they hopped as the ship came ashore, their boots splashing in the murky water. They were armed with spears, axes, perhaps even bows.

The people who lived near this particular inlet – the people whose goods these men had come to take – called the place *Duibhlinn* (black pool) in their Irish tongue, and the name would eventually stick. Its shores have long since been silted up and covered over; to stand upon the green grass of Dublin's Castle Gardens today is to stand upon the pool that gave the city its name.

The Vikings who stood there in 837 had not come alone. According to the contemporary *Annals of Ulster*, this fleet of 60 ships sailing up the River Liffey had a counterpart, a second Viking fleet of equal size moving up the River Boyne. Some 1,500 Vikings had arrived in Ireland, and they plundered the churches, forts, and homes in both river valleys. Their ferocity must have been genuine, but so, too, was the advantage of their vessels.

Archaeological recovery of Viking ships has enabled us to recognize their engineering excellence. The ships are constructed with overlapping planks built upon a strong keel: the result is a deeper, flatter, and longer hull with low sides and a stout central mast. The ships could thereby travel by sail or oar, and their shallow drafts meant that they could manoeuvre in small inlets and row up shallow rivers to strike locations well inland from where coastal raiding would be anticipated. Such was the knowledge of the craftsmen who made them that they even knew to split the timbers used in construction instead of sawing them: the wood, as a result, didn't dry out as easily, which enabled it to better flex when struck by heavy ocean waves.

Our sources don't name him directly, but many scholars assume that the Viking leader who stood upon the shores of that pool is the same man who is called by the *Annals of Ulster* 'chief of the foreigners' when he is reported killed by the Irish later that year. That man is named Saxoilbh in the Old Irish, though he almost assuredly spoke Old Norse and would have called himself Saxólfr in that tongue. Modern translations of the *Annals of Ulster* give his name as Saxolb.

Exactly where Saxolb came from – and where he and his men returned to – is a matter of some debate. The *Annals of Ulster* variously calls the raiders in 837 Northmen, foreigners, and heathens, which is hardly specific. To the Irish under their onslaught, it may have been difficult to sort out their geographical origins: in the 21st century sharp distinctions may be drawn between Danes and Norwegians, but in the ninth century such differences were not entirely clear to the non-Scandinavian world. Besides, it probably didn't much matter to the Irish where these Vikings came from. Specific ethnic identities weren't the issue. It was enough to know that they simply came from *elsewhere*. This was Us versus Them – except that what it meant to be 'Us' wasn't exactly stable, either. The Irish themselves had six overkings ruling over dozens of kingdoms, and in the coming years they would be more than willing to work with one group of Vikings to fight another group of Vikings or a rival Irish kingdom. When survival is at stake, identities can get quite malleable.

The raids on Ireland hadn't started with Saxolb, and they didn't end with his death in 837. So thoroughly were the Vikings ravaging the land, in fact, that by 841 they had switched from raiding to invading: Dublin became home for a community of the Northmen who utilized it as a base to carry out raids throughout the lands surrounding the Irish Sea. Many of these raids, it is now known, were carried out in order to feed a sea-spanning slave trade that connected to networks as far away as Russia.

The situation grew more complicated in 848, when the Irish annals report the killing in Leinster of a Viking earl named Thorir. This Viking leader is said to have been the deputy of the king of *Lochlann* – an unidentified king from an unidentifiable place (hence the italics). Scholars believe this foreign king is the same one said to have sent an army to Ireland the following year.

Then, in 851, there occurred the mass arrival of a large group of Vikings that the Irish sources call the 'dark foreigners'. Almost from the moment they set foot on Irish shores, they appear to be at war with those Vikings whom the annals begin calling the 'fair foreigners'. Scholars have spent an enormous amount of time arguing with one another about what 'dark' or 'fair' is meant to indicate – skin tone? hair colour? something about their armaments or their clothes? – and whether this identifier might help us understand where these various groups of foreigners came from. But recent scholarship suggests that this is to misunderstood the Irish entirely. The descriptors don't represent colour at all. In the Irish perspective, they distinguish the groups in terms of familiarity: 'dark' foreigners were the new Viking threat; 'fair' foreigners were the ones already known.[1] Beyond this, the context of our accounts seems to indicate that the 'dark' foreigners were those associated with the new incursion from *Lochlann*.

For a long time scholars assumed that the early medieval Irish word *Lochlann* referred to Norway, just as the modern Irish word *Lochlann* does, but it's been more recently theorized that while the men of *Lochlann* were broadly Scandinavian in origin, the location referred to was not specifically in Scandinavia but instead an independent Viking kingdom in Scotland, established in the early ninth century when Viking raiders overtook certainly the isles and potentially significant stretches of the north-western coast.[2] It was this kingdom, which was tied to Scandinavia by its genetics, tied to

Scotland by its logistics, and tied to no one by its politics, that had sent Thorir and the 'dark' foreigners to Ireland.[3]

The details that exist of the next couple of years are scanty at best – this whole period is among the least understood in the history of Ireland – but the image that emerges from the records is one of chaos as the two groups of Vikings and the many kingdoms of the Irish all struggled with one another for superiority.

Such was the situation when, in 853, Olaf, the son of the king of *Lochlann*, is said to have arrived in Ireland. All the Viking groups submitted to his rule, and even the Irish paid him tribute. He would come to be called Olaf Conung – the latter word marking him as king of the foreigners. Over the next two decades, in fact, the Irish chronicles speak of three such kings of the foreigners: Olaf, Ivar, and Auisle. According to an 11th-century saga woven into the *Fragmentary Annals of Ireland*, the three men were brothers, and their father – the king of *Lochlann* – was named Gofraid.[4] There is some reason to believe that they were indeed kinsmen, though whether they were blood-brothers or some other relation is perhaps unknowable at this point. Complicating things further, a fourth man, named Halfdan, is named in other sources as a 'brother' of Ivar. And the *Anglo-Saxon Chronicle* entry for 878, adding on, describes a raid carried out by a 'brother of Ivar and Halfdan' – yet another, unnamed 'brother' who cannot be Auisle (d. 867) or Olaf (d. 874).

This family and its descendants – whatever their relationship to each other – played a major role in driving much of the history of the British Isles until the coming of William the Conqueror. And though Olaf is the first of the family to appear in our story, it is the career of Ivar that we will follow most closely. Because only a few short years later, Ivar would make a name for himself as a war-leader for the Great Viking Army that very nearly ended England.

THE GREAT VIKING ARMY

At the outset of this book we learned how Egil Skallagrimson, that mighty Viking warrior-poet, composed a poem for the victorious King Athelstan in which he referred to 'three earls felled' in battle at

Brunanburh, 'all fallen under the kin of Ella'. Egil's Ella is believed to be a reference to the king who was killed by Ivar and the Great Viking Army in 866, when they entered Northumbria and seized its capital at York, setting in motion the war between the English and the Vikings that would lead to Brunanburh just over seven decades later.

Egil wasn't alone in seeing the significance of the Great Viking Army and the death of the Northumbrian king. By the 13th century there was a whole saga about it, called *The Tale of Ragnar's Sons*. According to this, Ella had captured a Norse leader named Ragnar Lodbrok and executed him by throwing him into a pit of venomous snakes. It was in response to this gruesome murder that Ragnar's sons – Ivar one of them – brought their massive army against England.

It's a wonderfully dramatic story, but it makes little sense. The pit of snakes sounds more like the work of a Bond villain than something one normally has at hand, and the numerous legends about Ragnar Lodbrok are ill at ease with themselves or with known historical facts. He may be a convenient figure for a television show like *The Vikings* to follow – weaving a single figure through an imagined history of the North – but a search for historical evidence of the man comes up rather short. He is, at best, semi-legendary.

Ella was real, though. So was his death at the hands of the Great Viking Army. But unlikely to be true is the concept that vengeance upon the Northumbrian king was the motivation for the Great Viking Army's invasion. For one thing, if killing a king in Northumbria was their aim, it would surely make the most sense for them to bring their longships ashore as close to their target as possible. They didn't.

Until 1672, a navigable arm of the North Sea called the Wantsum Channel ran from Richborough to Reculver, north-east of Sandwich, separating mainland Britain from the now-incorporated isle of Thanet. Richborough faces Thanet, and it had been the gateway to Britannia in Roman times: the Romans built an extraordinary arch here – the largest in the Roman Empire north of the Alps – and ruins of it likely still stood when William the Conqueror camped at it during the first weeks of the Norman Conquest in 1066. The fertile island of Thanet itself, according to the Venerable Bede, was the first land given by Vortigern to the original Germanic mercenaries when they had come during the Dark Ages. It was also where St Augustine of Canterbury first came ashore in 597 as he began the work of converting the pagan king of Kent to Christianity. By the ninth century the island and its monasteries had become a regular target and base of operations for Viking raiders, who used it to attack the descendants of those same Germanic peoples. So it was in 865: the Great Viking Army seized Thanet – which was some 200 miles away from Northumbria as the raven flies.

Some older historians have gone to some efforts to paint the Viking invaders as bloodthirsty killers, but there's little doubt that the invaded peoples had been just as efficiently killing each other long before the latest longships showed up upon their shores. In fact, fighting between the 'Anglo-Saxon' kingdoms had, by the time that the Great Viking Army arrived, reduced their number from seven to four. Wessex controlled the south of the island below the Severn–Thames line, along with a bulge of the former Essex up the east coast towards Ipswich. East Anglia was much as it is now. Northumbria held the lands south of the Scots to a line running roughly from Liverpool to the Humber. To Mercia went all the rest: the midlands from the Wash to Wales. In other words, it wasn't just that Kent wasn't Northumbria: it wasn't even *next to* Northumbria – East Anglian and Mercian lands lay between them.

At the head of this massive army, as we've already learned, were several leaders that our sources describe as brothers. In *The Tale of Ragnar's Sons*, of course, they're all the sons of Ragnar Lodbrok: Ivar the Boneless (so-called for reasons unknown),[5] Ubbe, Hvitserk, and Sigurd Snake-in-the-Eye (named for a mark on his iris). Another late saga, *The Tale of Ragnar Lodbrok*, lists the sons as Ivar the Boneless, Björn Ironside, Halfdan, Hvitserk, Sigurd Snake-in-the-Eye, and Ubbe. The more contemporary *Anglo-Saxon Chronicle* mentions Ivar and Ubbe, though later raids feature Halfdan and an unnamed brother (as seen above).

We have, then, a Viking leader named Ivar managing a great army in England with his brothers around the very time that a

Viking leader named Ivar had been managing the same in Ireland – a coincidence that would be rather remarkable despite the name being relatively common. More remarkable, though, the Irish Ivar falls out of the records in 865, at the very time when the English Ivar shows up; and English Ivar falls out of the records in 870, at the very time that the Irish Ivar once more shows up. It's impossible to *prove* they are the same man, but it would be one hell of a coincidence if they're not!

The biggest snag to identifying English Ivar and Irish Ivar as the same man, of course, is that the brothers and the named father – Gofraid vs Ragnar – don't quite line up. Whether this is due to failures in our sources or a misunderstood flexibility when it comes to kinship – or both – we may never know. The assumption here, at any rate, is that one way or another Ivar the Boneless is none other than Ivar of Ireland.

If it wasn't revenge for Ragnar Lodbrok – and given the distance to York it almost assuredly was nothing of the sort – then we don't know for certain what brought Ivar and the Great Viking Army to East Anglia in 865. A likely guess is that it was a combination of factors. Viking raids had been common around the shores of the North Sea for at least half a century. The 'E' text of the *Anglo-Saxon Chronicle* first describes their attacks with the arrival of three ships on English shores in 787:

> And in these days came first three ships of Northmen from Hordaland. The reeve, not knowing what they were, rode out and tried to convince them to go to the king's town. They killed him. These were the first ships of the Danish men who sought out the land of the English. [6]

It was, as the later chronicler notes, the start of things to come. Around 862, though, the Vikings may have been finding that some of their other conventional targets, like those of the Frankish shore, were becoming more difficult to attack. England may have seemed an increasingly enticing target in comparison. Added to this, there may also have been many Vikings who were spurred by their success in taking control of Ireland and wished to replicate the feat in England. Ivar would fit well in such a category.

We don't know the size of the army that was gathered. The *Anglo-Saxon Chronicle* simply calls it *se micel here*: the Great Army. It could have been several hundreds. It could have been several thousands. Whatever its size, it was apparently gathered from across the Viking world, including a major contingent with roots in Denmark, since many English sources also refer to it as the Great Danish Army – though, as we've already seen, geographical distinctions aren't terribly reliable when it comes to the identification of Vikings by their victims.

It's worth pausing for a moment here to reflect on what differences existed between these Viking invaders and the English they were invading. Contemporary sources tend to emphasize the separation between them, to underscore in every way possible how very 'other' the Vikings were. But no source is free from bias of one sort or another. For example, the *Anglo-Saxon Chronicle*, so central to any narrative of this period, may look like a simple history of dates and events, but it was initially composed in the court of King Alfred the Great of Wessex – who had more than a little cause to paint his Viking enemies in the worst of lights, as the next chapters will show. And the actual writers of that chronicle, as with so many of our surviving sources of the period, were also churchmen. Their bias can be seen in the alternative name they often used for the Vikings: Heathen. The English were Christian. The Vikings were not.

But even this religious separation can be misleading. It's true that St Augustine of Canterbury's mission to convert the English had been a resounding success. On Christmas Day 597 he led thousands of men and women from Kent in a mass baptism, and by 601 the king of Kent had converted. The progress of conversion appears to have been relatively steady, and so-called Anglo-Saxon paganism was largely squeezed out between subsequent Roman Christian missionaries from the south and Celtic Christian missionaries from the north – whose Christianity had survived over the centuries in places like Ireland and Iona. However, the fact that these kingdoms were Christian in name does not mean that their people were universally Christian in faith – and vice versa for the Vikings. There was (and still can be) a wide separation between the public affirmation of a religion and the private experience of it.

Beyond religion and language, it's remarkable how little might have separated the lives of the English and the Vikings – within social classes, at least. That is, farmers, fishermen, and tradesmen on the two sides would have recognized broad swathes of overlap in their behaviours and outlooks on the world. Farming is farming and fishing is fishing, after all. Likewise, the ruling classes of the two societies – classes that similarly identified themselves in terms of military experiences and capabilities – would have unquestionably recognized themselves in each other. Indeed, setting aside those religious and language differences, the English military elite likely would have had more points of social familiarity with their equivalent class of Vikings than they would have had with the common English under their rule. It's no surprise that Egil Skallagrimson was able to communicate his displeasure to King Athelstan in the hall after the battle of Brunanburh, and that the English king knew how to respond in turn. The warrior's gestures and the cultural expectations were intrinsically familiar.

A shared martial spirit and a wide body of cultural influences drive this familiarity. Indeed, to read Old English poetry is very often to read of the Viking world. As a most famous example, the hero of the greatest surviving epic in Old English, Beowulf, is a Geat – one of the two primary ethnic groups that would ultimately make up Sweden – whose adventures take him on a longship to Denmark. No matter what date we assume for the composition of the *Beowulf* epic – scholars have argued for dates between the sixth and tenth centuries – it's striking how Scandinavian it truly is. The same is true of the fragmentary Old English poem *Fight at Finnsburh* (a version of which is also told as an aside in *Beowulf*) and so much more. Again and again, we see in both cultures a social glorification of battle, especially within a ruling class that largely defined itself by prowess in combat. Even their weapons and strategies of war are more alike than different. In 1066, the exiled English earl of Northumbria, Tostig Godwinson, joined

with the Norwegian king, Harald Hardrada, in order to overthrow
Tostig's brother, King Harold II of England. Tostig had few men to
contribute to the cause, but he was nevertheless put in charge of an
entire wing of the army. And when Harald Hardrada died during
the battle of Stamford Bridge, it was Tostig who took control. Even
at that late date, whatever cultural differences existed between the
English earl and the Norwegian army they were not so sharp that
his command seemed strange – not one source blames the army's
defeat on a lack of common tactics or common experiences of war.

Despite the reality of such similarities, of course, the arrival of
the Great Viking Army in 865 was a very bad thing for the English.
Whether one accepted the threat as painted upon the moral
landscape of good and evil favoured by the churchmen or upon the
political landscape of power and control favoured by the elite, the
threat was unmistakably real. The most pressing expedience was
survival. This was a fight to stay alive.

The people of Kent responded to the surprise seizure of Thanet
by submitting to a tribute, a sum of money intended to buy
off the Vikings and prevent devastation. It wasn't enough. The
Vikings raided the coast of Kent before sailing north, across the
Thames estuary, to East Anglia. There, the king made peace with
the invaders by providing them with a large supply of horses –
essentially bribing them with the means to go and raid someone
else. The Vikings wintered over in Thetford. In the spring of 866
they were again on the move, headed north on land, while their
naval forces no doubt maintained a parallel track at sea.

Once more, if revenge in Northumbria was their motivation,
then they were in no hurry to see it through. Their march took
them north-west out of East Anglia, then up the eastern side of
Mercia. It wasn't until November of 866, more than a year after
their arrival, that they reached and seized the heart of Northumbria:
the former Roman fortified city of Eboracum. They called it Jorvik.

Today, we call it York. And the fight to control it would one day
bring men to the field of battle at Brunanburh.

Alfred and the Viking Conquest, 866–99

The future Alfred the Great was 16 years old and probably living in Winchester when the Great Viking Army arrived in distant East Anglia in 865. By the time he followed his three brothers onto the throne of Wessex in April 871, the Vikings were essentially at his door. And while his early years as king were marked largely by failure, he would persevere and manage to push his enemies back in extraordinary fashion. Along the way, he would make enormous changes to the political and military structures of England that would have an impact on where, when, and how Brunanburh would come to be.

THE TAKING OF YORK

But all that was yet to come when Ivar and the rest of the Great Viking Army reached York in 866. Founded by Roman legionaries on high ground above the confluence of the River Ouse and the River Foss, the city was already prosperous and powerful when the Vikings arrived. The Romans had left walls that were still usable – the Multangular Tower, part of the Roman fortifications, still stands today in York Museum Gardens – and there was a large and thriving populace. Where the magnificent York Minster now stands there was a smaller but still impressive stone church that had stood for some two centuries, replacing a wooden one that had been itself built upon the ruins of the original Roman encampment.

It's important to underscore that the Roman departure never meant the *erasure* of Rome. We can still see the traces of Roman presence across the countryside today, and Ivar, as he was entering York in 866, was two centuries closer to the building of the magnificent Colosseum in Rome than he was to our own day.

Exactly what he would have thought about Rome, we can't know. But he would not have been able to deny its physical presence all around him. Roman roads remained the arteries of both commerce and war across much of the former empire. Roman engineering still brought water, cleared sewage and underlay the structures of some of the biggest cities. Roman walls could still serve as protection. And even its abandoned magnificence could dominate the landscape. In the poem 'The Ruin', an anonymous English poet writing in the eighth or ninth century marvelled at the remnants of a Roman city – probably Bath – that had been empty for centuries:

> Wondrous are these wall-stones, wasted by fate,
> The courtyards crumpled, giants' works corrupted,
> The roofs tumbled down, towers in ruins,
> Frozen gate fractured, frost mixed in the mortar,
> Scarred storm-roofs raked and scored,
> Undone by the years. The earthen grip yokes
> Its proud builders, perished, long departed,
> The hard grasp of the grave, until a hundred generations
> Of people have passed. But this place outlasted,
> Grey with lichen, stained red,
> Knew one reign after another,
> Still stood after storms. The high arch has succumbed,
> But the wall-stone still stands in the winds ...[1]

As for the town surrounding the large Roman and post-Roman constructions in York, a series of archaeological digs which took place between 1976 and 1981 (when an abandoned factory was torn down to be replaced by the Coppergate Shopping Centre) recovered more than 40,000 artefacts of everyday medieval life, along with the remains of numerous buildings, homes, and shops. These finds have given us enormous insights into what the town was like when the Vikings arrived in the ninth century: largely wooden buildings with thatched roofs lining packed-dirt streets that too often turned to mud.

Medieval York had a fortified enclosure, but it was hardly the large stone walls now seen in the city. It took no great siege for York to fall to Ivar and the Great Viking Army. Northumbria was at the moment of their arrival fractured by contesting claimants for its throne, and for all that we can tell no one was able to make much of a defence of the city as a result. The city was among the most prized jewels in the north, and it appears the Vikings more or less walked in and seized it.

By March of 867, the rivals for the Northumbrian throne had set aside their differences in order to attack the Vikings, but they were soundly defeated in battle. It was in this fight that Ella of Northumbria was killed. He was one of those rival claimants for the throne. More than that, he was the man that the later Norse legends accused of killing Ragnar Lodbrok so elaborately that he had set the Vikings on this rather meandering walk towards vengeance. As for Ella's own death, the stories embellished this, too. A poem written by Sigvat Thordarson between 1020 and 1038 hints at a gruesome fate:

And Ella's back –
By that one, Ivar,
Who sat at York –
Was cut with the eagle.[2]

Later Norse writers would explain just what they thought was meant: a ritual execution that would come to be called the 'blood eagle'. As *The Tale of Ragnar's Sons* describes it:

Now they had an eagle carved on Ella's back and then cut all of the ribs from the spine, so that the lungs were pulled out.[3]

The lungs, being pulled from the back, were thus apparently meant to be the bloody 'wings' of the eagle.

Such a means of execution is, in a word, horrifying. It also may not be real. The accounts of it are not contemporary to the events being described, and they come from sources interested in making the horrors more lurid. Beyond this problem, the blood eagle would be, because of its gruesomeness, a strange means of execution since the victim would be likely to die long before the torture was carried out in full. As a post-mortem desecration of the body for display it *might* be possible, though if it was at all a recognized cultural phenomenon there ought to be more evidence of it than there is.[4] That there was a practice of somehow marking the condemned with the sign of an eagle – omitting the business about the lungs – *might* be possible, but even that might be just a misunderstanding of early poetic descriptions of dead bodies on the field of battle: many of the defeated were left face-down, and their exposed backs are where carrion fowl like eagles would begin to feed. As we have already seen, a focus on the battle-feast was common.

Whether or not it would be better or worse that someone, in the absence of the actual practice, *imagined* the horror of the blood eagle is a question I leave to the reader.

* * *

One way or another, the king of Northumbria was dead. York had fallen. And Ivar and the Great Viking Army were just getting started.

The Vikings marched south, back into Mercia, and wintered over in Nottingham. Bribed off by the Mercians, they returned to York for the winter of 868–69. The following spring, they headed even further south, and in November they once more killed a king. This time it was Edmund of East Anglia. Like Ella, his death would become the stuff of legend, as stories would be told of the Vikings testing whether his Christian god would protect him. They tied him up. They shot arrows at him. He died.

Such an ending is more reasonable than a blood eagle, but there's still reason to doubt its validity. The *Anglo-Saxon*

Chronicle, composed a couple of decades after his death, tells us that the Vikings were wintering in Thetford when Edmund fought them and lost: 'the Danish took the victory, and killed the king and conquered all that land'.[5] Though initially buried somewhere nearby, his remains would be transferred to the town of Beadoriceworth, which quickly took the name by which it's now known: Bury St Edmunds. The elaborate stories of Edmund's Christian-mocking death don't appear until there was already the beginning of a cult honouring him as a martyred saint. How that cult began – whether because the stories of his martyrdom have a basis in truth or for any number of other reasons – we just don't know. Such was its popularity, however, that in 925 King Athelstan himself would help found a religious community in connection with his saintly remains.

If Ivar the Boneless was Ivar of Ireland – as I believe he was – then it was not long after Edmund's death that the Viking leader turned his eyes elsewhere. By 870, he had joined his brother Olaf Conung in laying siege to Dumbarton Rock. That massive fortress, then apparently the royal seat of an independent Briton kingdom that would become known as Strathclyde, fell after a four-month siege when its water supply gave out. In 871, the two Viking leaders returned to Dublin with a fleet of 200 ships loaded with booty and captives – most of the latter intended for the slave markets.

VICTORY AT ETHANDUN

In the same year that Dumbarton Rock fell, the future Alfred the Great was crowned king of Wessex. That winter, the Great Viking Army was wintering in London.

For the next years the Vikings split their forces into northern and southern contingents, but they lost none of their potency. When brought to battle, they won more than they lost, and they appear to have moved across the land with relative impunity. More than once Alfred and other leaders tried to buy them off, but the Vikings appear to have seen better profit in continuing their raids against ineffective adversaries.

By 877, the last kingdom remaining free of Viking influence was Alfred's Wessex, and his hold on it was greatly diminished. Alfred spent that winter in Chippenham, and in early January a small Viking force surprised him there and forced him to flee to Athelney. The legend that at that point his kingdom was reduced to this single spot of land in the Somerset marshes may be an exaggeration – but not by much. England was in real threat of being snuffed out in its infancy.

There was time enough for one last gasp. And whether Alfred was aware of it or not, his adversaries were weakened. The immediate army facing him was led by a Viking named Guthrum, who was dealing with political problems of his own as the Great Viking Army had spent years breaking apart, changing shape, and losing increasing numbers of men who had turned from roving raids to permanent settlement. That spring, Alfred sent word out to the surrounding territories, summoning men to gather for a fight. Since the very beginning of the Middle Ages, the English king had held the right to call out able-bodied freemen in times of emergency. They were farmers and tradesmen, among other occupations, so how much they trained for war – assuming they trained at all – remains an open question. Outside of wartime, they could also be levied for major construction works, such as the building of fortifications or the building of bridges. Whether in war or peace, these men constituted a general levied militia called the *fyrd*. In May, the levy of three shires met Guthrum in open battle at a place called Ethandun.

For a long time, Ethandun was a battlefield regarded as nearly as lost as that of Brunanburh, though the search radius for Alfred's victory was far smaller than it was for Athelstan's, and the candidates far fewer. Today, there is little doubt among historians that Alfred's Ethandun is modern Edington, in Wiltshire.

The sources don't provide enough information to even begin to speculate on how the battle happened. We can neither pin it to the landscape nor imagine its tactics beyond the generalities of the period. Men lined up across an open space. Boasts were made and insults were shouted – poetic, profane, or maybe both. Shield-walls advanced and met. The fallen dead became the battleground for the living.

Alfred carried the day. Guthrum and the Vikings fled to a stronghold – probably Chippenham – but within two weeks they'd been starved out and forced to submit to what is often called the Treaty of Wedmore, though it was probably a verbal agreement rather than a formal written accord. It was, in any case, peace: Alfred took hostages from among the Vikings, who agreed to leave Wessex. Guthrum himself agreed to be baptized by Alfred's own hand. The Viking leader took the Christian name of Athelstan – meaning 'noble' or 'princely stone' – and accepted ceremonial adoption as the king's son. It was the same name that Alfred's grandson would be given just two decades later.

Alfred's reputation rests strongly on this victory over his enemies. Some 13 years after the Great Viking Army had come, it had at last been turned back.

Like the Anglo-Saxon Invasion that wasn't really an invasion, this idea isn't true in the way that most people understand it to be true. The Vikings were turned back from Wessex, but not from England. We don't know exactly when the more formal written agreement, today called the Treaty of Alfred and Guthrum, was signed, but it consists of just five basic clauses. One of these defines the worth of a man's life, either Englishman or Dane, as equal. Another defines the judicial principles through which charges could be levied against those of status. Two more govern the purchase and movement of slaves, horse, and oxen between the two sides. All of these are interesting to the historian, of course, but of particular note for us here is the first clause, which delineates the boundary between the holdings of King Alfred and those of King Guthrum, as he is termed. This line runs along the Thames, then along the Lea to its source. From there, a straight line would run to Bedford and thence along the Ouse to Watling Street. Roughly speaking, this drew a line across England from just north of London in the east to Chester in the west. Everything north and east of the line belonged to Guthrum and the Vikings. Everything south and west belonged to Alfred and the English.[6]

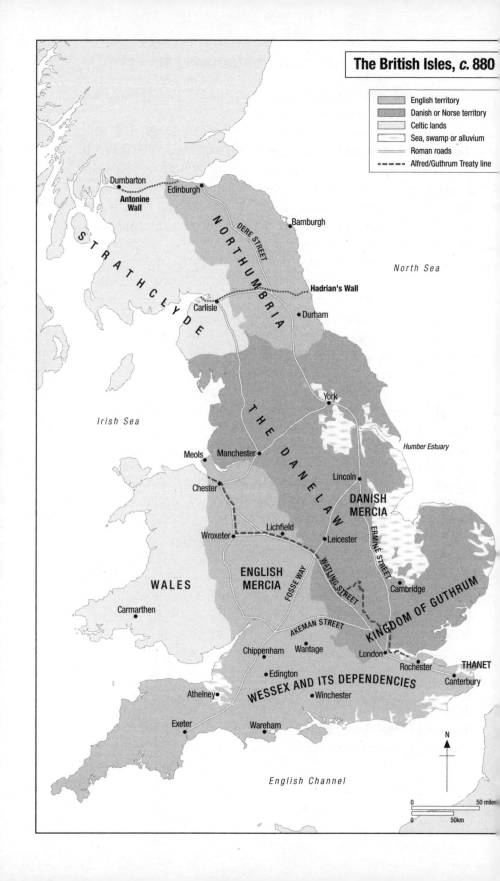

The British Isles, *c.* 880

Legend:
- English territory
- Danish or Norse territory
- Celtic lands
- Sea, swamp or alluvium
- Roman roads
- Alfred/Guthrum Treaty line

Dumbarton
Antonine Wall
Edinburgh
Bamburgh

North Sea

N O R T H U M B R I A

DERE STREET

Hadrian's Wall

S T R A T H C L Y D E

Carlisle
Durham

Irish Sea

York

T H E   D A N E L A W

Humber Estuary

Meols   Manchester

Lincoln

Chester

DANISH MERCIA

ERMINE STREET

Wroxeter
Lichfield
Leicester

WALES

ENGLISH MERCIA

FOSSE WAY

WATLING STREET

Cambridge

K I N G D O M   O F   G U T H R U M

Carmarthen

AKEMAN STREET

Chippenham   Wantage

London

Rochester   **THANET**

Canterbury

Edington

WESSEX AND ITS DEPENDENCIES

Athelney   Winchester

Exeter   Wareham

English Channel

N

0   50 miles
0   50km

So it's true that Alfred brought peace to his lands, but it's also true that in the same stroke he legitimated Viking control over much of what would today be considered part of England. The borders of this Viking-controlled land would vary over time, but its presence would be a consistent, looming threat over the future of the English for generations. Because the Vikings were identified as Danes – whether or not they were all, in our sense, Danish – the land would eventually come to be called the Danelaw, for it was under the laws of the Danes.

THE OTHER ENGLISH KINGDOM

Wessex had not been the only English kingdom still standing in the south in 878, but by the time that Alfred was making his treaty that other kingdom, Mercia, had been subsumed by Alfred. What happened?

It should be said at the outset that Mercia had seen more than its fair share of troubles as the Great Viking Army moved in and out of its territory – as early, we may recall, as its march to York. According to the *Anglo-Saxon Chronicle*, things took a turn for the disastrous in the year 874:

> Here the raiding-army went from [the kingdom of] Lindsey to Repton and took winter-quarters there, and drove the king Burhred [of Mercia] over the sea 22 years after he had the kingdom; and conquered all that land. And he went to Rome and settled there ... And the same year they granted that the kingdom of Mercia to be held by a foolish king's thegn [Ceolwulf II], and he swore them oaths and granted hostages, that it should be ready for them whichever day they might want it, and he himself should be ready with all who would follow him, at the service of the raiding-army.[7]

King Ceolwulf II of Mercia is painted as little more than a Viking puppet here, but once more the bias of our sources comes into play. The *Anglo-Saxon Chronicle* was written in the court of Alfred, who was brother-in-law to the exiled King Burhred. It was also written some years after Alfred had taken control over what was left of Mercia – after he had formally given roughly half that kingdom's lands to the Vikings. Indeed, because the creation of the Danelaw so greatly reduced the kingdom of Mercia, historians have generally dated the Treaty of Alfred and Guthrum to the years after 879, after King Ceolwulf II was gone. There is, in other words, more than one reason to think that Alfred's court historians might have tried to hide the truth of what was going on between Wessex and Mercia at the time.

Despite their efforts, a glimpse of the truth came to light in 2015, with the discovery of the Watlington Hoard in Oxfordshire. Among its 186 silver coins, apparently buried by Vikings after Guthrum's defeat at Ethandun in 878, were several picturing both Alfred and Ceolwulf II seated side by side. Their representation as equals on the same coins, struck over the course of several years at several different mints, indicates that a firm and formal alliance had been made between the two rulers and their kingdoms. It seems remarkably unlikely that such a coalition would be built between the king of Wessex and a Viking puppet.

Ceolwulf II's reign appears to have ended in 879. Whether he died or was deposed is unknown, but Alfred's interest in destroying his reputation *could* indicate the involvement of Wessex in getting rid of him. One way or another, lordship over the remaining lands of Mercia had passed to a man named Athelred, who in 881 was defeated in battle by Welsh forces at the battle of the Conwy. For several years Mercia had been trying to seize control over parts of Wales in the west – perhaps in part driven by their losses of lands to the Viking in the East – and there had been some early successes. Most notably, Ceolwulf II had killed the Welsh leader Rhodri the Great in battle in 877. But Athelred's loss in 881 was a heavy blow for the Mercians. Welsh leaders turned to Alfred for support, and a diminished Athelred accepted Alfred as his king. Athelred, now lord of the Mercians, was given the hand of Alfred's eldest daughter, Aethelflaed. This lady of the Mercians would prove a powerful figure in the years to come.

Alfred the Great may have begun his rule as the king of Wessex, but by around 886 he had taken a far grander title: king of the Anglo-Saxons. It had been a remarkable rise from the swamps of Athelney. However, once again, we should be wary of crowning the king with a greater victory than he had really achieved. What he called himself and how the people viewed him need hardly have been the same thing.[8]

A DIFFERENT WAY OF WAR

Alfred was no fool. He knew how close he had come to destruction in the months before Ethandun, and he rightly identified a number of reasons why he had had such difficulties against his enemies.

There was, perhaps, no greater reason than this: the individual combat tactics of the Vikings and the English might have been as similar as the roots of their cultures, but their larger war strategies were markedly different. Insofar as there were understood 'rules' of war – *expectations* would surely be the better word – the Viking arrival in the eighth century had broken them in shocking ways.[9] First, while pre-Viking Britain had seen more than its share of battles, these were largely fought between combatants whose origins were known. When a neighbouring kingdom attacked, the trail to vengeance was clear. More often than not, the very route of its advance could likely be followed. The Vikings, however, through the advantage of their ships, shattered this expectation. Their assaults were, in modern terms, amphibious: a water landing, a fast raid, and a water retreat. What's more, the Vikings were able to bring these amphibious attacks well inland of the expected targets on the coast, erasing traditional zones of battle and replacing them with a broader sense of a society under threat. And wherever they struck, whenever they struck, the only trail they left behind was the blood washed out with the tide. We've already seen the uncertainty in our sources over where the Vikings came from: a frustrating hurdle for the modern historian but a frightening horror for the medieval victim. Where could vengeance be sought when the enemy's origins weren't even known?

Even when it came to more extensive, land-based attacks like those faced by King Alfred, the Vikings had more often than not engaged in hit-and-run tactics. The simple fact once more gives lie to the popular conception of bloodthirsty Vikings. Rather than seeking conflict, these warriors generally preferred to avoid it. They wanted riches – whether land, slaves, gold, or goods – and all things being equal, the easiest and most efficient way they could get them was preferred. Battles were to be avoided.

History books tend to focus so much on battles that it can be easy to miss the fact that the best generals most often try to avoid them. They know that battles, except under the most perfect conditions of surprise, are inherently unpredictable. Dumb luck can destroy the finest of plans. The Bible speaks truth in this, at least: 'the race is not to the swift, nor the battle to the strong, nor bread to the wise, nor riches to the learned, nor favour to the skilful: but time and chance in all.'[10]

The Vikings that Alfred had fought understood this, and it dictated *how* they fought. Rather than marshalling troops for pitched battles with uncertain outcomes, the Vikings had perfected the art of the hit-and-run. Even when it came to invasion, the Vikings were largely disinclined to campaign in the open field through force of numbers. Instead, they opportunistically seized soft targets that they could turn into hard ones: locations that were lightly defended but easily defensible. Once fortified, these became bases of operation for further raids and offensives that could be carried out on favourable terms. If chance could change everything, then the Vikings were determined to leave as little as possible to its whim.

This type of warfare is imminently sensible: maximizing impact while minimizing risk. And yet, it must be said, it was not the same kind of military strategy that had been deployed by the English prior to Alfred the Great. Their armies had been largely reactive. When an attack came, the men would ride in from the surrounding regions, gathering in response. Maintaining the readiness of armed forces is an expensive proposition that can be hard to bear even when needed during times of war. In times of peace this social weight can seem far more burdensome. Measured only in economic terms, there was enormous benefit to decentralizing the armed forces in the days before the Vikings came. After the Vikings came, however, the risks of this decentralization were put into stark relief. By the time the army had gathered in response to an attack, there was a good chance the attackers were gone. Simply catching the enemy had become a challenge.

It's of little surprise, then, that when Alfred took stock of his kingdom's situation, he focused on a new strategy. He had bought time by his treaty with Guthrum, but he knew the Vikings had broken treaties before. He knew, too, that even if he had convinced one wolf to stay away, there were others that might be more than willing to assault his flock. To solve these problems, Alfred reorganized the military of his kingdom. Importantly, he built a series of fortified positions that were garrisoned by a standing army. Such a fortification was called a *burh*, which means 'fortified place'.

Although it probably dates from the reign of his son, a surviving administrative document called the *Burghal Hideage* suggests that roughly 33 of these burhs were dedicated to the defence of the kingdom. A look at this contemporary list shows how varied these fortified places might be. Some were old Roman towns with old Roman walls, while others were even older Iron Age earthworks that were re-occupied and repaired. Still others were far more recent in construction: their ditches, ramparts, and other fortifications were apparently built in response to Alfred's awareness that they were needed to fill a gap in this strategic network of defence.

Such endeavours weren't undertaken without great cost and effort. There is clear evidence that many nobles were less than happy with the financial outlay that was necessary not just for constructing the burhs but also for providing them with the standing garrisons that were necessary for the maintenance of the forts and their defence.

Though the immediate years after Ethandun were relatively quiet, Alfred's foresight in remodelling the defence of his kingdom was proven as raids increased after the death of Guthrum in 889. In the mid-890s, Alfred's system was put to a hard test when a fleet of over 300 ships brought two Viking armies ashore in Kent.

For several years the English and the Vikings jockeyed for position, with Alfred's forces again and again getting the upper hand before the invaders fled to friendly lands.

In 898, one year before his death, Alfred's son, who would follow him to the throne as Edward the Elder, had a son of his own. It is a strange coincidence of history that this baby boy was given the same name that the defeated Guthrum had taken on his baptism. After all, this child would grow up to become the king who took the field at Brunanburh and defeated the great coalition of Vikings and Scots and other enemies who had come to erase England from the map once and for all.

His name was Athelstan.

4

The Gathering Storm, 900–24

By the time of his death in 899, Alfred had built new systems of taxation to support the growing centralized apparatus of his kingdom's government and the costs of advances, like the burhs, that would defend it against its adversaries. The political and military might of the English was undoubtedly on the rise. For the other powers that vied for control of the British Isles, this new strength was an unquestionable threat – though as the tenth century began none of them seemed immediately prepared to do anything about it.

Across the Irish Sea, for instance, the Vikings of Ireland were about to see their control over the island broken. Ivar, at the height of his power, returned to Ireland from his successful conquest of Dumbarton Rock in 871. Just two years later, the 'king of the Norsemen of all Ireland and Britain', as the *Annals of Ulster* called him, was dead.[1]

Thanks to Ivar and his brothers, Dublin had become a prosperous and bustling port, in large measure because it was by now the largest centre for slave trading in Western Europe. This made it a tantalizing prize for those seeking power or riches – or both. In the last quarter of the ninth century, at least eight men had been or had claimed to have been kings of Dublin, and their struggles with one another had greatly weakened the kingdom's military strength. Many of these were members of the Uí Ímair, the dynasty of Ivar, which consisted of complicated and unclear family relationships. In the year 900, the latest of these Dublin kings was probably another Ivar, who appears to have been a grandson of Ivar the Boneless.

THE DUBLIN REFUGEES

Meanwhile, the native Irish had gathered strength to stand against the Vikings. In 902, the kings of Brega and Leinster joined forces and succeeded in expelling this latest Ivar – and no doubt much of the Viking elite with him – from Dublin. As the *Annals of Ulster* relates:

> The heathens were driven from Ireland, i.e. from the fortress of Áth Cliath [at Dublin]... and they abandoned a good number of their ships, and escaped half dead after they had been wounded and broken.[2]

Archaeology hasn't turned up evidence of anything quite so dramatic: the city doesn't show any period of complete abandonment across the period. It may be, then, that the exile was mainly confined to the ruling Viking elite, and that people continued to live in the town under the new Irish leadership. Still, even if they had succeeded only in kicking out the leaders, it was an enormous success for the Irish ... that quickly became a problem for their neighbours around the Irish Sea.

Ivar and his fellow exiles took to their ships and scattered. Some may have sailed to the Isle of Man, some to France, others to Scandinavia or places even farther afield. It appears that many of them, however, including Ivar himself, sailed north for the Hebrides and other lands that might well have been the *Lochlann* from which his grandfather had originally come. He was there the following year, fighting with King Constantine II of Scotland. In 904, the *Annals of Ulster* records Ivar's death at the hands of Scots. This same year the *Chronicle of the Kings of Alba* names Constantine the victor against Vikings at a battle at Strathearn – it can be assumed that this, then, is where Ivar died.

Another group of Dublin refugees settled along the coast of Lancashire, where there were already a number of small Viking communities. It may be that their arrival led to the raising of a force that intended to push up the River Ribble in an attempt to re-occupy York. Their failure to do so is among the explanations for the existence of the Cuerdale Hoard, found near Preston in 1840: at almost 9,000 items, the largest Viking hoard ever found in the British Isles.

Meanwhile, it appears that another contingent of these exiled Vikings sailed east from Dublin, following the prevailing winds across the Irish Sea. In 903 the *Annals of Wales* (often referred to by its Latin name, *Annales Cambriae*) reports that a group of Vikings under the leadership of a man named Ingimund tried to settle on the island of Anglesey before the Welsh fought them off. These same Vikings then took to ship once again and headed further east along the northern coast of Wales. According to the *Fragmentary Annals of Ireland*, they reached the lands of English Mercia.

As we saw in the previous chapter, the last king of Mercia had been Ceolwulf II: after he lost the crown – whether he was deposed or died is unknown – a man named Athelred became lord of the Mercians, answering to Alfred as king of the English. As part of this arrangement, Athelred was given the hand of Alfred's daughter, Aethelflaed. Her husband didn't die until 911, but there are indications that the lady of the Mercians was more or less running the place as early as 902. The *Fragmentary Annals of Ireland* says it was to Aethelflaed that Ingimund came when he asked to settle in Mercia.

Given the widespread evidence of a significant Scandinavian presence in the area, historians have long believed that this settlement would have been located on the northern stretches of the Wirral, the peninsula between the estuaries of the Dee and Mersey rivers. Whether there were pre-existent Scandinavian settlements as part of the trading network between Mercia and the rest of the population around the Irish Sea is unknown. Place-name evidence – a strong initial clue to the existence of what might be called Viking Wirral – only goes as far back as the first recording of a name. For much of England, this 'first citation' is the 1086 Domesday Book of William the Conqueror. Still, it seems a good assumption that Ingimund and his people settled on the Wirral, probably in the north-western portions of the peninsula, in or around the important trading centre of Meols or West Kirby – both of which have Norse names.

If Aethelflaed demanded something in exchange for refugee settlement on Mercian lands, there is no record of it. Many have speculated that a deal was struck in which the Viking settlers agreed to act as a buffer or perhaps even a direct line of defence against other Viking groups. After all, Aethelflaed's most immediate concern would no doubt be that the Viking presence would grow as word spread of this new opportunity for settlement: the welcome drip could become a decidedly unwelcome flood. Not only would uncontrolled Viking migration into Mercia threaten her own lands, it might also threaten all that Alfred had gained: the River Mersey was one of the waterways that could help connect the Viking operations in and around the North Sea with their former stronghold at York. We've already seen that a Viking army might well have made just such an advance up the Ribble in these same years. The threat was real.

Around 907, a localized version of the *Anglo-Saxon Chronicle* called the *Mercian Register* informs us that Aethelflaed restored the Roman walls of Chester, the nearest large city to the Wirral, which had been briefly taken by the Vikings in 893.[3] It's extremely tempting to connect this defensive work to the presence of Ingimund and his people: a deal that was sweet on their initial arrival might have already been going sour. Those who wish to connect the re-fortification of Chester to the Vikings often point to an unusually long entry in the *Fragmentary Annals of Ireland* that describes an enormous battle around this time – waged by Ingimund and his allies against Aethelflaed at the very walls of Chester. This work is often called *Ingimund's Saga*.

According to *Ingimund's Saga*, Aethelflaed – wrongly called the 'Queen of the Saxons' – was in a position of leadership because her 'king' husband was ill. She had initially offered Ingimund and his fellow 'Norwegians' – as the source calls this particular group of a Vikings – the lands in the northern parts of the Wirral, but soon enough Ingimund had his eye on better lands closer to Chester. He proceeded to lead his people into an agreement with other

Norwegians as well as 'Danes' in nearby lands: Ingimund would ask Aethelflaed for better places to settle, but if she didn't agree they would attack as a unified force, along with a great many Irish fosterlings who were among them. Unfortunately for the alliance, Aethelflaed sniffed out the agreement, and she responded by filling Chester with fighting men. When Aethelflaed refused Ingimund's requests, the combined Viking forces made ready for battle.

So far, one might say, so possible – though there are no English records of a land grant between the Mercians and Ingimund or records of any major conflict between them over the matter. Still, given the lack of information regarding Wirral history in general, we could at least posit that *something* like this might have happened.

The same cannot be said for the details that *Ingimund's Saga* provides about the ensuing battle. The Mercian plan, it reports, was to offer battle directly in front of Chester's open city gates. At a signal, the Mercian armies would feign retreat into the city: hopefully, this would prompt the Vikings to think the city was theirs for the taking. In triumph, they would leave their organized lines and give chase. Once they were inside the city, however, the gates would be slammed shut behind them. Trapped, they would be destroyed by a group of Mercian horsemen who lay in wait. As the battle began, this plan was executed to perfection, and 'complete slaughter' ensued among the ambushed Vikings. Those who were still outside the city were enraged at the deaths of their companions, and they began a siege, setting up hurdles (protective wooden pickets) and attempting to undermine the walls.

In response, *Ingimund's Saga* says, the Mercian leaders convinced the Irish among their attackers to betray their allies. The Irish agreed, ambushing the Danes at the very moment that they had set aside their weapons to give oaths that they would reward the Irish for their help. As for the rest of the alliance:

Yet the Norwegians, the other part of the army, were under the hurdles, mining under the wall. The Saxons, joined by the Irish, hurled huge boulders down, crushing the hurdles over their heads. The Norwegians responded by putting large supports under the hurdles. The Saxons then gathered up all the ale and water in the town and boiled it in cauldrons that they then dumped upon the men under the hurdles, scalding their skin off their bodies. The Norwegians responded by spreading hides on top of the hurdles. The Saxons then threw all the beehives there were in the town on top of the besiegers. The Norwegians couldn't even move their hands and their feet because of the number of bees stinging them. After that they gave up the city and left. Not much later there was fighting again ...[4]

This whole sequence is enormously dramatic ... and almost certainly false. Why the elaborate – and easy to backfire – ruse of the open city gates? How likely would it be that the assembled Mercian fighters were trained well enough to manage such a retreat? Why would a contingent on horseback be used during the ambush in the city, where the tight confines of streets and buildings would make it difficult for mounted men to operate? How likely was it that the Mercians were even trained to fight on horseback? How could the Mercians have communicated with the Irish component of the besiegers so effectively? For that matter, how likely were the Vikings to engage in a siege of this kind in the first place?

Worse still, there is no evidence of a complex siege occurring at Chester: not in the city's extensive archaeology and not in the sources. Aside from the rather inventive *Ingimund's Saga*, all we have is the casual mention in a chronicle that its walls were refortified in 907 – which, for all we know, could have been just as much a reaction to rumblings from Wales as to rumblings on the Wirral. That was, after all, the presumed reason for a similar strengthening of the fortifications at Shrewsbury in 901.

In fact, looking across the first few decades of the tenth century, it is evident that any effort to view the geopolitical situation along a Viking/English axis over-simplifies a far more complex reality. The Welsh were a constant presence in the west, and in addition to apparently independent Viking leaders like Ingimund in the north-west, there were other kings still around, and some of them were Vikings, too.

RIVAL POWERS

In the years since its arrival the Great Viking Army had splintered and changed. Waves of immigrants had moved into the lands that had been taken by force or diplomacy: as we have seen, beyond the immediate frontier east and north of England stood what would eventually be called the Danelaw. The border between these lands and those of the English shifted over time, but it was always porous. The lines between states in our modern world are precisely defined, but this has hardly been the standard throughout history. For the most part, ancient and medieval borders were set at the level of who most immediately controlled each village, farm, and field. Cultural intermingling was inevitable, and it had lasting impacts on the English language, giving us a host of loanwords with Viking origins, like *egg*.

Militarily, however, the Danelaw was at this moment relatively weak. Alfred had spent the last years of the ninth century centralizing power in the English kingdom, but Guthrum had managed no equal endeavour in Viking lands. Across the Danelaw there were a number of regional powers – a Danish East Anglia, a Danish Mercia, and a Danish Northumbria with its prized city of York. They didn't always work in concert, and it would be easy to overstate even their individual unity. The power of Danish Mercia, for instance, was built around earls ruling in what became known as the Five Boroughs: Derby, Leicester, Lincoln, Nottingham, and Stamford. In short, while raiding parties still harried the English border from various points in the various Viking-held lands, a consolidated army wasn't gathered to push back against the English until the destructive campaign that resulted in the battle of Tettenhall in 910.

This campaign appears to have been a retaliation. In 909, Aethelflaed and King Edward had joined forces to make a month-plus incursion straight through Danish Mercia into Lindsey, during which they recovered the remains of Oswald, a Northumbrian king turned saint, from Bardney Abbey in Lincolnshire. In response to this English offensive, the Vikings gathered an army and sailed it up the Severn into the heart of Mercia. This route, as well as the choice of target, suggests that Vikings from the west coast of England might have joined their counterparts from Northumbria. The damage they collectively did was apparently significant, but the systems of response that Alfred had begun worked well: forces from Wessex and Mercia quickly gathered against the threat. They caught the Viking army before it could make its way back to friendly territory, and battle ensued near Wolverhampton at a place called variously Tettenhall or Wednesfield. The *Anglo-Saxon Chronicle* reports the deaths of multiple Viking kings alongside thousands of their men. Included in their number were the rulers of Danish Northumbria: it appears that York was now under the influence of the Christian leaders of English Northumbria, centred on Bamburgh.

Lord Athelred of Mercia died in 911. It's likely that Aethelflaed had already been ruling Mercia in all but name, but after his death she was officially the lady of the Mercians. And for the half-dozen years after Tettenhall – indeed, probably because of it – she joined her brother, King Edward, in overseeing an enormous expansion of the system of burhs and other fortified sites that their father Alfred had begun:

- 910: *Bremesburh* (unidentified)
- 912: *Scergeat* (unidentified), Bridgnorth, and Hertford
- 913: Tamworth and Stafford
- 914: Eddisbury, Warwick, and Buckingham
- 915: Bedford, Chirbury, Runcorn, and *Weardbyrig* (unidentified, perhaps in the West Midlands)
- 916: Maldon

Taken together, these English fortifications may seem defensive, and very often scholars have accordingly regarded the two rulers as building a 'ring' that would protect English holdings. In truth, however, their construction was often *offensive*, pushing the frontier outward. As William the Conqueror and the Normans would later do, the English were claiming their territory by establishing

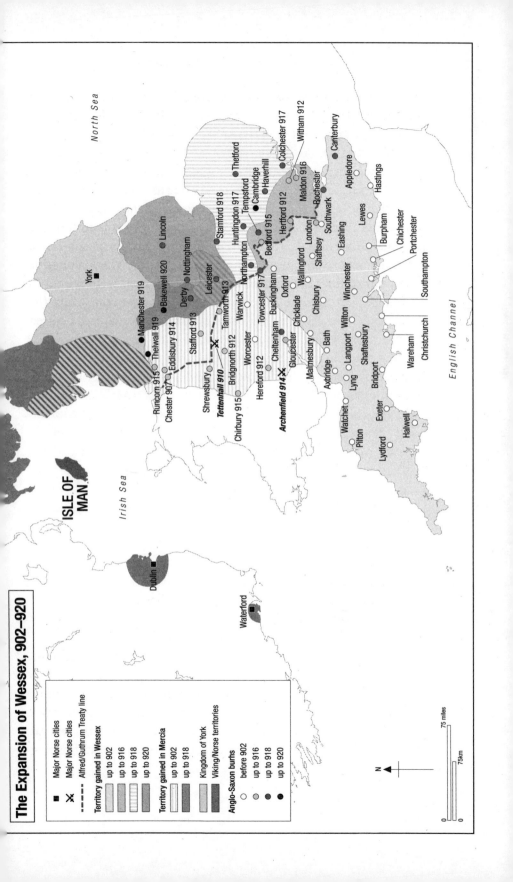

The Expansion of Wessex, 902–920

Major Norse cities ■
Major Norse cities ✕

Alfred/Guthrum Treaty line ---

Territory gained in Wessex
up to 902
up to 916
up to 918
up to 920

Territory gained in Mercia
up to 902
up to 918

Kingdom of York

Viking/Norse territories

Anglo-Saxon burhs
before 902 ○
up to 916 ○
up to 918 ●
up to 920 ●

North Sea

Irish Sea

English Channel

ISLE OF MAN

Dublin ■

Waterford ■

York ■

Manchester 919
Thelwall 919
Runcorn 915
Chester 907
Eddisbury 914
Bakewell 920
Lincoln
Derby
Nottingham
Leicester
Stafford 913
Shrewsbury
Tettenhall 910 ✕
Tamworth 913
Bridgnorth 912
Chirbury 915
Archenfield 914 ✕
Warwick
Worcester
Hereford 912
Cheltenham
Gloucester
Towcester 917
Buckingham
Northampton
Bedford 915
Hertford 912
London
Stamford 918
Huntingdon 917
Tempsford
Cambridge
Haverhill
Thetford
Maldon 916
Witham 912
Colchester 917
Rochester
Southwark
Canterbury
Appledore
Hastings
Lewes
Burpham
Chichester
Portchester
Southampton
Eashing
Winchester
Wilton
Wallingford
Oxford
Cricklade
Chisbury
Shaftsey
Malmesbury
Bath
Axbridge
Shaftesbury
Langport
Lyng
Bridport
Watchet
Pilton
Exeter
Lydford
Halwell
Wareham
Christchurch

N

0 ⊢ 75 miles
0 ⊢ 75km

fortified centres of control that extended their reach. The burhs didn't mark the line of the English frontier as it currently was, but as the English hoped it would be.

Perhaps inevitably, this era of English expansion meant that the English were also more and more willing to campaign, as they had in 909, into the territory of their adversaries. The year 916, for instance, saw a significant Mercian expedition against the Welsh that reached into Brecknockshire to destroy a royal holding near Llangorse Lake. The next year saw an even greater accomplishment as Aethelflaed's armies captured Derby, one of the Five Boroughs. It was, put simply, an extraordinary triumph.

Watching all of this, almost assuredly accompanying his aunt on her military campaigns against the Vikings, was Edward's eldest son, the future King Athelstan. He was in 917 perhaps in his early 20s, and, for reasons explained in the next chapter, he had grown up in the Mercian court. It must have been an amazing time and place to come of age. The Danelaw was shuddering. Dublin and York, those great jewels in the crown of Ivar's dynasty, had both fallen. The Viking threat that had defined generations of English life must have seemed to be in permanent retreat.

There was no way for anyone to know that in just two short decades the Vikings would roar back and bring the English – and the now King Athelstan – to the brink of disaster at Brunanburh.

THE VIKING RESURGENCE

In 917, just as Aethelflaed was triumphant over one group of Vikings in Derby, another group was on the move: two fleets showed up in Ireland, both of them led by 'grandsons' from the dynasty of Ivar the Boneless. Sihtric Caech and Ragnall were probably brothers or cousins of the more recent Ivar who had been driven from Dublin in 902. There's a decent chance that they had all been together on the boats that had sailed away. Now, 15 years later, it seems they were determined to restore their family's lands.

Sihtric brought his fleet ashore near the border of Leinster. Ragnall brought his into Waterford. Alex Woolf has observed that the enormity of the forces they brought to bear is shown in 'an almost unparalleled display of military unity among the Irish' in response.[5] The Irish kings tried to fight off the invaders, but at the battle of Cenn Fuait the king of Leinster was slain along with a number of other key leaders. Not long afterwards, the Vikings entered Dublin. Sihtric would once more be its king.

No one should have been surprised that the family's eyes now turned to York. Just one year later, the ships were cutting the waves again: Ragnall sailed for Northumbria with yet another 'grandson' of Ivar, named Guthfrith.

The political landscape that awaited them in the north was anything but simple. Northumbria, since the days of Ivar the Boneless, had been roughly split between a northern region governed by the English in Bamburgh and a southern region governed by the Vikings in York. Since Tettenhall, however, the English had dominated much of the combined Northumbria. In 918, it was under the rule of a man named Ealdred.

But Northumbria wasn't the only northern power. North of these lands was the kingdom that would become Scotland, a conglomeration of Gaels and Picts who had been politically united by their opposition to the Vikings who for generations had raided and – especially among the isles and along the western coasts – invaded their lands. The king of Scotland in 918 was still Constantine II. His predecessor, Donald II, had fought hard against the Vikings and probably was killed by them near Dunnotar Castle, south of Aberdeen. Constantine, too, had seen his share of war: he and his Scots had fought back a number of Viking incursions, including the one in which the younger Ivar had lost his life after his exile from Dublin.

The sacking of Dumbarton Rock by Ivar the Boneless in 870 appears to have wounded but not killed the realm of Britons that was centred on the valley of the River Clyde – south of Scotland and west of Northumbria. Previously called Alt Clut (their name for the Rock), this kingdom was after 870 called Strathclyde or Cumbria, and its seat was apparently moved to Govan. We know far less than we would like to about the kingdom in this period. Even the name of their king in 918 isn't known for certain, though many historians have suggested that it was a young Owain, who would later join Constantine of Scotland and the Viking Guthfrith's son as unlikely allies at Brunanburh.

And aside from these major political powers, there were also the Viking settlements that had been putting down roots along the west coast, from the Wirral on up. It is even possible that Ragnall held some of these lands himself. There are so few accounts of the period. Though some of them shine bright, there's no question that the history of western Northumbria – despite being literally in the middle of everything – remains in darkness.

So perhaps it's not surprising that the route Ragnall and Guthfrith took to reach Northumbria is frustratingly uncertain. The first definitive mention of their army comes from the *History of Saint Cuthbert*, which says that Ragnall 'came with a great multitude of ships' and seized the territory of Ealdred, the aforementioned English leader of Northumbria. Ealdred, defeated or at least frightened into flight, sought refuge in the court of Constantine.[6] What pact was struck between them isn't known, but it was apparently enough to bring the Scots south – further afield than ever before – to push out the latest Viking threat. The Scots met the Vikings at the battle of Corbridge, which the *Annals of Ulster* firmly locates on the banks of the Tyne.[7] This riverside location has been enough for most historians to assume that a Viking fleet had sailed around the north or south of England to enter the Tyne from the east. That said, the spotty nature of our records for the area means that we cannot completely discount the possibility that the multitude of ships had made a main landing among the friendly ports of the west coast and then made an overland march along one of the several routes that had been in use since Roman times if not before. Given a fight on the Tyne, with York untaken, we might assume either a landing on the Clyde, followed by a march towards the Firth on the Roman road shadowing the Antonine Wall, or a landing on the Solway Firth, followed by a march along the Roman road running alongside Hadrian's Wall. Of the two, the route by Hadrian's Wall seems more likely. Corbridge sits at the point where this Roman road meets with Dere Street – for centuries the main route for those travelling south from Scotland to York. The same kind of scheme – sail up a western river, then march overland east towards York – had apparently been attempted by the Dublin refugees after 902. The river then was the Ribble, and the Roman road the one through Skipton to Ilkley to meet Dere Street at Boroughbridge. Whether or not Ragnall or Guthfrith were with that ill-fated group, they would have known of their intentions and could well have chosen a similar path.

One way or another, everyone came together at Corbridge. Two Viking leaders were slain in the initial engagements, but a surprise attack by Ragnall's men drove the Scots from the field. Each side had reason to claim victory, but the inescapable truth is that when it was over the Scots went home – and Ragnall took hold of York.

DEATH OF A LADY

To the south, Aethelflaed hadn't been resting on the laurels of her victory at Derby. Not long afterwards she secured a *second* of the Five Boroughs – Leicester this time – without bloodshed: the Danes there had seemingly decided that a future submitting to the lady of the Mercians was better than a future fighting against her.

Aethelflaed was at the height of her power, and others around the island were taking notice. The *Mercian Register* states that after Ragnall and his Vikings had driven Ealdred from Northumbria, a segment of the population of York began negotiating with Aethelflaed for the protection of the city. This may be because they were Christians fearing pagan rule under Ragnall, though one cannot rule out the possibility of other economic or political reasons for the gesture.

It's hard to imagine what future events might have looked like if the lady of the Mercians had succeeded in acquiring York and taking control over so much of Northumbria. The *Fragmentary Annals of Ireland* states that she had made a pact with the kings of Scotland and Strathclyde, and that she herself had led a Mercian army at

Corbridge. Placing her at that battle seems extremely unlikely. The idea that she was involved with making gestures towards an alliance across the north, however, cannot be dismissed entirely out of hand. Had she held York – and potentially had agreements with other northern realms at the same time – Mercia's fortunes relative to those of Wessex might have been reversed.

As it was, however, Aethelflaed unexpectedly died in June 918, before any agreement could be made with the Christian Vikings of York over the fate of Northumbria's jewel. Ragnall took his prize. And by the end of the year, King Edward – who had recently had an enormous success of his own in retaking Danish East Anglia – performed what might be described as a *coup d'état*: 'three weeks before Christmas', according to the *Anglo-Saxon Chronicle*, he deposed his older sister's daughter and heir, Aelfwynn. What became of her after she was led into Wessex isn't known. It is likely she was sent to a convent, though she has been attached to a range of women with the same name in the succeeding years in an effort to 'find' her. In her place, King Edward appears to have placed his son Athelstan in charge of Mercia. What the Mercians thought of all this, our largely Wessex-based sources don't bother to say. If there had been doubts among the island's other leaders about the expansionist agenda of Wessex, Edward's actions in Mercia must have put them to rest.

First, though, Edward would need to secure his newly won or newly annexed holdings from any northern threat. To secure Mercia's western border, Edward received the submission of the three most prominent kings of Wales, all grandsons of the famous Rhodri Mawr: Hywel and Clydog, sons of Cadell and rulers of Dyfed and Seisyllwg in the south, and Idwal, son of Anarawd and ruler of Gwynedd in the north. To secure Mercia's northern border – which now faced Ragnall's holdings from the Isle of Man to York – and also no doubt to stamp down any local English resistance to his rule, he built new fortifications at Manchester and Thelwall in 919, then a second fortification at Nottingham in 920 – this time on what had been the Viking side of the River Trent – along with one at Bakewell. As this latest construction was being completed, the *Anglo-Saxon Chronicle* describes a meeting between many of the major political powers in Britain:

> And then the king of Scots and all the nation of Scots chose [Edward] as father and lord; and [so also did] Ragnall and Eadwulf's sons and all those who live in Northumbria, both English and Danish and Norwegians and others; and also the king of the Strathclyde Britons and all the Strathclyde Britons.[8]

We have already seen how the *Anglo-Saxon Chronicle* is greatly biased towards the English – and often the Wessex court in particular – and this scene is no exception: whatever happened at Bakewell, it was almost assuredly not a formal submission to Edward by the kings of Scotland, Northumbria, and Strathclyde. It is far more likely that it was a subtler diplomatic agreement. Edward had ample reason to fear that Ragnall would move south into the old territories of the Danelaw, which were still newly won; he also must have feared that the Scots and the Strathclyde Britons might enter into an active alliance with a Viking-controlled York. In return for promises not to take such actions, Ragnall could have gained assurance that Constantine and Ealdred would not again attack him from the north and that York would pass without contention to his heirs. Constantine achieved security for Scotland in the wake of his defeat at Ragnall's hands, and the still-unnamed king of Strathclyde caught between them all surely welcomed the chance to ensure the survival of his holdings in what was an increasingly contested part of the Isles. That something like this was the truth of the matter at Bakewell might well be indicated by the events surrounding Ragnall's death later that year. His cousin (or brother) Sihtric left Dublin to succeed (peacefully, by all accounts) to the throne of Northumbria. Heading in the other direction was Guthfrith, the other grandson of Ivar who had accompanied Ragnall from Ireland. Guthfrith now became the king of Dublin. At no point in this game of musical thrones did Edward, Constantine, or anyone else make a move against this latest incarnation of Viking Northumbria.

Despite the propagandist spin of the English chronicler, no one was accepting the over-lordship of an English king at Bakewell. Edward was definitely flexing his muscles – siting the agreement at the newly constructed English fortress in the north was an unmistakable gesture – but essentially everyone was agreeing to the new status quo: stand down, fighters back to their corners. Edward was in no position to demand more, and there was no reason for the other leaders to offer it.

Edward's own position was still tenuous, after all, especially when it came to his annexed lands in Mercia. In 921, he built a fortification at Rhuddlan, which could command against the Vikings and Welsh alike. Just a few years later, in fact, the Mercians in Chester revolted against Edward's rule, joined in their defiance by the nearby Welsh. Noticeably, and important to remember for the archaeology to come, there is no mention of the local Scandinavian communities on the Wirral taking part. In response, the king personally rode out to restore order. And while no sources mention it, he might well have been wounded in the action: on 17 July 924, the rebellion only just put down, Edward died at nearby Farndon in Cheshire.

Brunanburh was only 13 years away.

The Rise of Athelstan, 924–34

In the year 1125, a monk named William of Malmesbury put the finishing touches on a book he called *The Deeds of the English Kings*. The book chronicled English history from 449 to 1120, and it would go on to be tremendously influential on the development of English culture, even if some parts of William's narrative – like his magnificent tales of King Arthur – are better assigned to myth than to history as we understand it today.

Still, we owe an enormous debt to William, perhaps most especially for those passages in which he preserved what appears to be reliable information from sources now lost to us. A significant example is his account of King Athelstan, which, William tells us, derives from 'a certain old book' he had found. Numerous unsuccessful attempts have been made to find traces of this book, with a number of scholars doubting its existence, but the general consensus is that he was working from a tenth-century source of *some* kind.[1]

One of the stories William found in this now-lost source features a very young Athelstan, who had been born around 894 to Alfred the Great's son, Edward the Elder. Athelstan's mother was named Ecgwynn, and next to nothing is known of her. William reports rumours of her being Edward's consort, but such whispers have the ring of later attempts at character assassination that probably date from Athelstan's competition with his brother Aelfweard for their father's crown.

At any rate, William tells us a story about how the child Athelstan – who would have been four or five years old – was called before Alfred, who formally presented his grandson with a scarlet cloak, a belt studded with gems, and a 'Saxon' sword with a gilded scabbard. Scholars have generally agreed that such a ceremony probably happened – with gratitude to William for preserving this detail that would otherwise have been lost – but there's been little agreement on what it actually meant. It could have been simply the gift of a magnanimous grandfather to a precious grandson, but the symbolic nature of those gifts and the formality with which they were presented appears to speak to something more: a statement about the young lad's right to rule. Certainly this is the context of the story for William, who relates it as part of Alfred's hopes that Athelstan's eventual rule would be prosperous.

Edward followed his father onto the throne. Not long afterwards, Edward was married a second time. Had Athelstan's mother died? Had she been set aside for political reasons? We don't know. All we have is the mention of the second marriage – and the report that Athelstan was sent from the court of Wessex to the court of Mercia around the same time. Edward's second marriage was fruitful, and it's doubtful that the queen wanted the child of her husband's previous marriage to stand in the way of her own sons by the king taking the throne.

In Mercia, Athelstan was raised by his aunt, Aethelflaed. His life there was surely quite comfortable. Even if his going there was intended as an exile of some kind – and, again, we have no idea if it was – he was still a potential heir to the throne. As it would have been said in his native Old English language, he was an æðeling, a prince. Among other things, this status meant that he was given the finest education possible. Old English had been his first language, but it seems likely that he knew a fair bit of Latin and perhaps even picked up a smattering of the Norse spoken by the Vikings with whom his family had so often been in contact.

He also would have received a great deal of training in warfare. Family connections – what we think of as 'royal blood' – might make a person eligible to wear a crown in Athelstan's day, but eligibility wasn't inevitability. Leadership was about practical worth, and this worth was often defined by skill in war. Athelstan was born eligible for the crown, but if he was to be worthy of wearing it he needed to know how to fight. This meant training in the tactics of how to command troops on the battlefield, the strategy of how to deploy an army on campaign, and the logistics to keep fighting men fed, watered, and moving. He would eventually have known not just how to wield the sword Alfred gave him, but how it was made, bought, and paid for – and when and how to place such a weapon into a soldier's hands.

From all indications, Athelstan excelled in his many studies. Perhaps precocious signs of this had been apparent to his grandfather. Perhaps this was why he had given Athelstan gifts symbolic of a king.

TAKING THE CROWN

As we've already seen, King Edward the Elder died at Farndon in 924, shortly after putting down a Mercian–Welsh revolt in Chester. Athelstan, who was around 30 years old, was probably with his father on the campaign. There is some reason to suspect that Athelstan had been nominally in charge of Mercia after the death of his aunt in 918.

Athelstan was Edward's eldest son, so the Mercians quickly proclaimed him king. The West Saxons, however, proclaimed as king Aelfweard, Edward's second-eldest son – but the eldest from his second wife and the first one born to Edward as a reigning king. For a moment it seemed that the brief unity of Mercia and Wessex would be broken, but Aelfweard followed his father to the grave within a month. About a year later, on 4 September 925, Athelstan was crowned king. His choice to hold this coronation at Kingston-upon-Thames, situated on the traditional border between Mercia and Wessex, surely symbolized his intention to rule a unified realm:

rex Saxonum et Anglorum, as he was named in his first charters, 'king of the Saxons and Angles'.[2]

It was at this time that an intricate acrostic poem was composed in Athelstan's honour. The first letters of its eight lines combine to form the name 'Adalstan' (i.e. Athelstan), while the last letters in the lines form the name 'Iohannes' (i.e. John), and it twice makes plays on the meaning of the fact that the king's name means 'noble stone' in Old English.

'**A**rchalis' clamare, triumuir, nomine 'Sax**I**'.
Diue tuo fors prognossim feliciter aeu**O**:
'**A**ugusta' Samu- cernentis 'rupis' eris -el**H**,
Laruales forti beliales robure contr**A**.
Saepe seges messem fecunda prenotat altam; i**N**.
Tutis solandum petrinum solibus agme**N**.
Amplius amplificare sacra sophismatis arc**E**.
Nomina orto- petas donet, precor, inclita -doxu**S**.

You, prince, are called by the name of 'sovereign stone'.
Look happily on this prophecy for your age:
You shall be the 'noble rock' of Samuel the Seer,
[Standing] with mighty strength against devilish demons.
Often an abundant cornfield foretells a great harvest; in
Peaceful days your stone mass is to be softened.
You are more abundantly endowed with the holy eminence of
    learning.
I pray that you may seek, and the Glorious One may grant, the
    [fulfilment implied in your] royal names.[3]

As the previous chapters have shown, the political map of Britain had been anything but stable since the departure of Rome. But the last years of the reign of King Edward had been extraordinary even by that chaotic standard.

As Athelstan took the throne, he could claim virtually all the lands south of the Humber and east of Offa's Dyke. Immediately north of the Humber, Sihtric ruled much of Northumbria from York.

North-east of this, centred on Bamburgh, was whatever Ealdred had left of English Northumbria. To its north-west was the small Briton kingdom of Strathclyde, probably ruled by Owain. North of them all was Scotland, with its long-ruling King Constantine II. And west of Offa's Dyke, Wales was divided into a number of competing kingdoms. There were smaller pockets of political concern here and there – the Norse community on the Wirral, for instance, probably maintained some local autonomy despite being under the English crown – but in terms of the main players on the board, this was it.

This was it for Britain, that is. King Athelstan was, as we have seen, an educated man. He knew the history of his people, which meant he knew only too well that Ireland could not be ignored. The Irish themselves hadn't shown much interest in crossing the sea, but the Viking successors to Ivar most certainly had. Athelstan's main concern in that regard would have been Guthfrith, who had become the king of Dublin when his brother or cousin Sihtric had left it to take the throne in York.

INITIAL DIPLOMACY

The immediate question, though, was what to do with Northumbria. Of the distant Heptarchy of 'Anglo-Saxon' kingdoms, this realm alone, close on his northern border, stood completely beyond Athelstan's grasp. When he at last took hold of Mercia and Wessex in 925, Athelstan immediately looked to York, making a move against his rivals that would – in just over a decade – help lead to their powerful retaliation against him at Brunanburh.

In hindsight, this first move was both predictable and ingenious. Growing up in Mercia, Athelstan had seen how deftly his aunt's marriage to the ruler of Mercia had brought peace between the two realms. He had seen how Aethelflaed had gone from an outsider wife to rule in her own name. He had seen how his father had skilfully manipulated the take-over of Mercia after her death. Now he would try to do the same. Within months, he had struck an agreement to marry his full-blood sister to Sihtric, the king of Northumbria. According to the 'D' version of the *Anglo-Saxon*

Chronicle, Sihtric came to Tamworth to celebrate the marriage on 30 January 926. That the event took place deep inside Athelstan's territory – rather than at a more neutral border location – could be a sign of the relative strength of the two kings, though this can't be known for sure. As part of the terms of the marriage, the two kings promised to support each other and not to help the other's enemies. For Athelstan, the agreement would secure his northern border, while also, he hoped, preventing an attack from Sihtric's relatives in Ireland to the west.

Nor was this Athelstan's only move of marital diplomacy. Before he had become king, one of his half-sisters had already married Charles the Simple, king of the West Franks, and Athelstan himself would eventually send another to marry the future Holy Roman Emperor Otto the Great. ·In the same year that the arrangement was made with Sihtric, Athelstan arranged to marry another sister to Hugh, a Frankish duke. William of Malmesbury tells us that the duke sent a number of holy and imperial relics to help convince the English king to agree to this particular marriage. The list of items includes spices, jewels, swift horses, an extraordinary vase, and still more:

> ... the sword of Constantine the Great, inscribed with the ancient owner's name in golden letters, with one of the iron spikes used to crucify our Lord affixed to the scabbard with golden fastenings; ... the lance of Charlemagne ... said to be the same one that pierced our Lord's side [upon the Cross]; ... the banner of St Maurice, martyr and general of the Theban legion, which Charlemagne used in battle in Spain; ... a crown, precious from its quantity of gold, but more so for its jewels; ... a piece of the Holy Cross enclosed in crystal, so clear that one can look through the stone and see its colour and size; ... a small piece also of the crown of thorns, enclosed in a similar manner, which, in mockery of His kingship, the raving soldiers placed on our Lord's sacred head.[4]

The list, taken in its entirety, is fairly astonishing. It's also somewhat suspect in that it looks much like traditions of gifts that took place within Ottonian Saxony, which could have been confused with those gifts passed to Athelstan from the Continent.[5] Even so, there is no question regarding the international relationship with which these supposed gifts were associated. Athelstan's sister was indeed sent to Hugh.

There is also no question regarding Athelstan's longing for relics of imperial or religious significance. His devotion to the trade of holy relics in particular was well known across the Continent. And at least one of the items William lists – the crystal enclosing a sliver of the Holy Cross – might have actually made its way to England. Among the holdings of the British Museum is a rock crystal, engraved with the scene of the Crucifixion, with what appears to be a slot for a relic in its back.[6] Though nothing is known of its history before 1867, it appears to be Frankish, and it fits William's description of Hugh's gift to Athelstan – and that of a relic he was later described as wearing during the battle of Brunanburh.

YORK AND EAMONT BRIDGE

Whether or not Athelstan modelled his Northumbrian plan on what happened in Mercia, it succeeded beyond his hopes. It took Edward more than 30 years after Aethelflaed's marriage to annex Mercia. Athelstan's annexation of Northumbria took less than two.

Sihtric died in 927. Guthfrith, in Ireland, assumed the throne would be his. He accordingly planned to leave his throne in Dublin for a greater throne in Northumbria, just as his kinsman had done. Athelstan, in England, assumed something quite different: his sister, like Aethelflaed in Mercia, had the right to rule through her marriage to the former ruler. It was a collision between models of kingship, but speed would be the arbiter between them: Athelstan marched north much faster than Guthfrith sailed there. By the time the Viking claimant had arrived, Athelstan had already secured York. Whether for reasons of security – his sister hadn't had enough time to build the strong relationships Aethelflaed had built in Mercia – or personal ambition, the English king demanded that the people of Northumbria submit to his crown. They did.

What happened next was unquestionably important, and just as unquestionably uncertain.

According to William of Malmesbury, Athelstan learned that at least two of Sihtric's kin had escaped York – either one a potential focal point for resistance to English rule. One of the men had gone north, and the English king sent messengers to the kings of Scotland and Strathclyde demanding that the fugitive be given over to the English on threat of war. In response, the two northern kings met Athelstan near the monastery of Dacre in Penrith, where they submitted to Athelstan's authority.

The 'D' version of the *Anglo-Saxon Chronicle* places this meeting about six miles east of Dacre, at Eamont Bridge. It claims that Athelstan here accepted under his rule 'all the kings who were in this island' – that is, he received the submission of not two but *four* of his royal peers in Britain: Constantine II of Scotland, Owain of Strathclyde, Hywel Dda of Wales, and Ealdred of Bamburgh. 'And they confirmed peace with pledges and with oaths', the chronicle says, and they furthermore 'forbade all devil-worship'.[7] The chronicle also provides us with a date: 12 July 927. For many people, it is this, not the arrival of the 'Anglo-Saxons', that marks the date and place for the birth of England.

As with the supposed submissions to Edward at Bakewell some years earlier, we have to be cautious in our attempts to separate fact from fiction here. If Athelstan had indeed received submission from all four kings, Eamont Bridge was an extraordinary moment. But what would have been in it for these other kings? Bakewell, we've seen, was likely more of an acceptance of a new status quo in Britain. That could definitely be called a kind of victory for the English – they had been the party who had expanded their territory the most – and it certainly makes sense that total dominance is the story they would choose to tell posterity. Perhaps it was the story they told themselves. But status quo is hardly the same as the formal submission of one crown to another.

Much the same, it seems to me, is the case with Eamont Bridge. Athelstan had seized new lands, and he had made a show of force to defend that seizure. No one was in a position to tell him no.

Their greatest concern was that he not threaten their own lands, as well. The 'submission' was, once again, an agreement to a new status quo. The northern leaders wouldn't contest Athelstan's claim on Northumbria. In return, the English king wouldn't pursue a claim into their lands.

William's report of Athelstan threatening his fellow kings presumably has a seed of truth in that the English king no doubt wanted to impress upon them his magnanimity in not marching further, but – again, like Edward – he probably wasn't truly in the position to be marching hither and yon fighting all the world. His main interest was to secure his new gains.

That Northumbria wasn't yet secure seems logical – state administrations don't start and stop on a sixpence – and it's also borne out by William's report that as soon as the agreements were made at Eamont Bridge Athelstan had to turn back towards York. Guthfrith, one of the fugitive kinsmen of Sihtric that Athelstan had sought from the northern kings, had escaped. As feared, he had raised enough of a resistance to besiege York, claiming what he believed to be his rightful throne. Athelstan fought off Guthfrith, then supposedly dismantled many of the Viking fortifications there in order to help ensure that the great northern city couldn't be used against him should he lose control of it once more. Only much later did the elusive Guthfrith surrender himself to Athelstan's mercy. According to William, the king magnanimously gave him gifts and sent him back to sea. This Guthfrith, no doubt, was Sihtric's kinsman who had left the throne of Dublin to claim the throne at York, only to be beaten to it by Athelstan.

To that end, Irish sources inform us that Guthfrith was six months away from Dublin before he returned from Britain, a gap that William's sequence fits well. A failed assault also neatly fits with our expectation that the Viking claim to York was a lingering concern for Athelstan. Again, for all the power he wanted to present at Eamont Bridge, he really just needed to secure his newly expanded realm. Any agreement made with the other kings was made with exactly this security in mind: Athelstan needed to ensure that his new northern border would not be breached. For their part, Constantine and Owain (and Ealdred of Bamburgh if he indeed was there) needed to know that English ambitions stopped at that same border.

The very location of the meeting strongly points to just such a mutual desire. A good guess is that Athelstan stayed in the monastic lodgings at Dacre while the formal pledges took place at nearby Eamont, the river crossing somewhere on a mile stretch of fertile meadows where the rivers Eamont and Lowther meander close beside one another before joining streams today. To the west, this space is marked by two ancient henges – Mayburgh and King Arthur's Round Table. To the east, it is marked by the ruins of the Roman fort at Brougham Castle.

Historians have largely ignored the importance of this Roman past to what was unfolding here. As we've already seen, Roman roads remained the main conduits of transportation in the tenth century. If Hadrian's Wall is considered a kind of rough border between north and south (at least in Roman terms if not in Athelstan's mind in 927), then there were only two main roads connecting this frontier to the lands south of it. The first road was Dere Street, which crossed the Tyne at Corbridge before running to York. In political terms for Athelstan, this eastern road ran to Ealdred of Bamburgh's lands and then into those of Constantine in Scotland. The second road ran from Carlisle on the Solway Firth to Brougham, where it split into three different routes to York, Manchester, and Ravenglass. In political terms, this was the road to the lands of Owain of Strathclyde, as well as to the western shores of the Irish Sea and its many Viking threats. To meet at Eamont, beside Brougham, meant to meet upon one of the two main avenues of entry that any northern attack on the English would presumably take. What's more, it was to meet upon the Strathclyde–Viking road more specifically. Scotland and Bamburgh were essential players in maintaining any new status quo, but it was the threat of *this* road, *that* potential political mix, that was clearly on Athelstan's mind.

At Brunanburh, such a threat would become a reality.

Fig. 1. At the bottom of this section of the Bayeux Tapestry, opportunistic survivors can be seen stripping the dead of their possessions. Such desolate battlefield scenes were clearly also in the mind of the poet of *The Battle of Brunanburh*. (Wikimedia Commons, CC0 1.0)

Fig. 2. The Pillar of Eliseg, an important source in our efforts to unlock the secrets of Britain's Dark Ages. (Wolfgang Sauber, CC BY-SA 3.0)

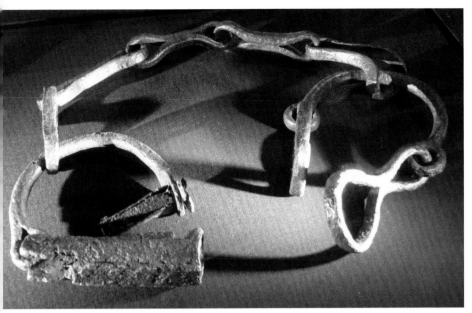

Fig. 4. A slave chain from the Viking period, exhibited at the Archäologisches Landesmuseum Mecklenburg-Vorpommern. Many of the Viking raids on Ireland in the ninth century were carried out in order to feed this growing trade. (Wolfgang Sauber, CC BY-SA 4.0)

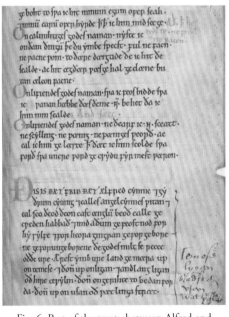

Fig. 5. The Alfred Jewel, made for King Alfred the Great and found in a field just a few miles away from Athelney Abbey, now housed in the Ashmolean Museum. (Photo by Ashmolean Museum/Heritage Images/Getty Images)

Fig. 6. Part of the treaty between Alfred and Guthrum, which set out the boundaries between their holdings, copied into Cambridge, Corpus Christi College, MS 383, fol. 57r. (Parker Library, Corpus Christi College, Cambridge)

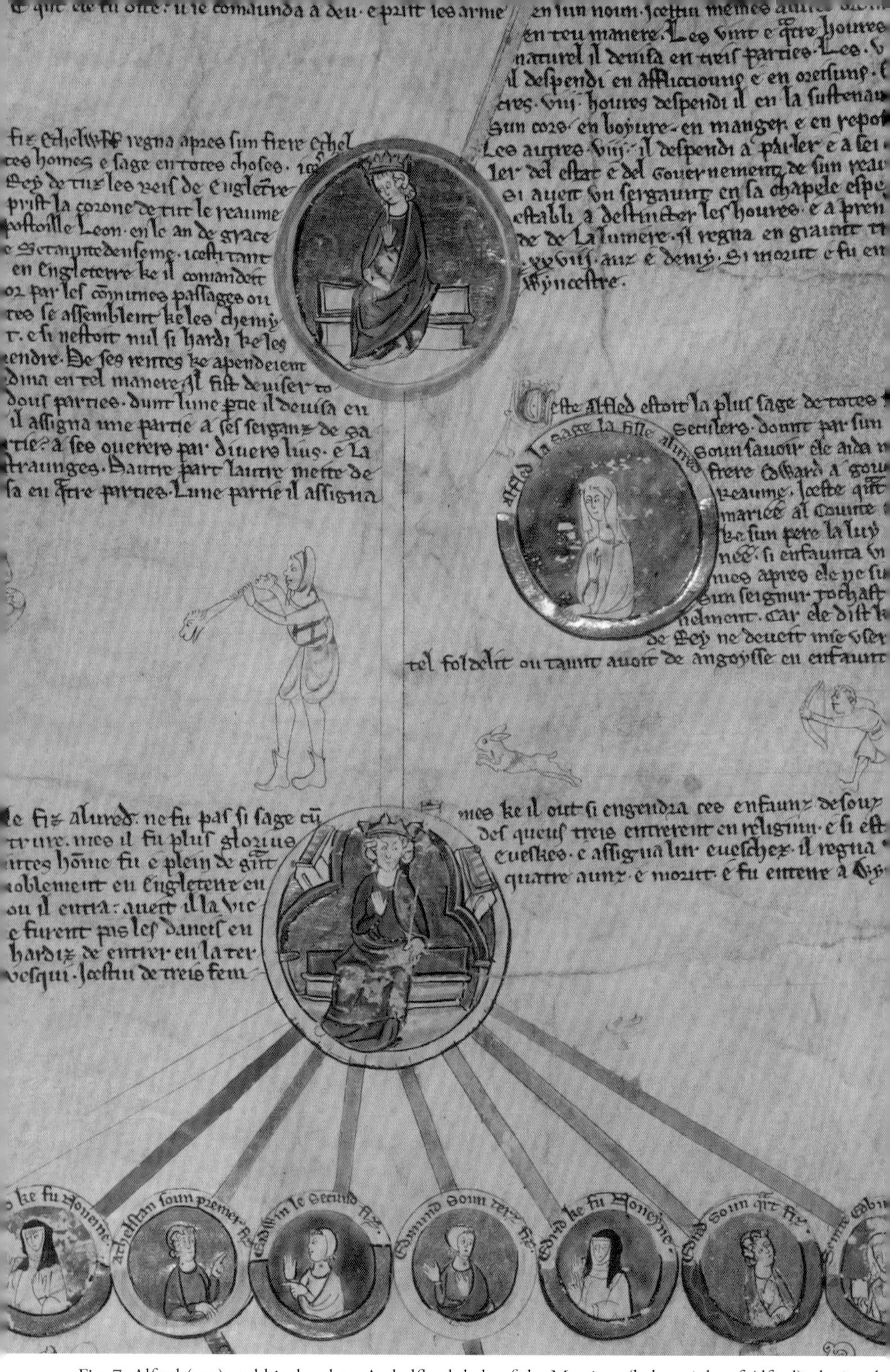

Fig. 7. Alfred (top) and his daughter Aethelflaed, lady of the Mercians (below right of Alfred), depicted in a 13th-century manuscript now housed in the British Library. (© British Library Board. All Rights Reserved / Bridgeman Images)

Fig. 8. Among the thousands of pieces recovered from the Cuerdale Hoard, the largest Viking hoard ever found in the British Isles, is this beautiful tenth-century brooch. (Photo by Universal History Archive/Universal Images Group via Getty Images)

Fig. 9. Also found in Lancashire, the Silverdale Hoard is believed to have been deposited in the tenth century, around the same time as the Cuerdale Hoard. (Image by Ian Richardson, Portable Antiquities Scheme, CC BY-SA 2.0)

Fig. 10. A modern re-enactor depicting a Viking warrior of some status in the early tenth century. (Richard Cutts. Model: Andrew Quick of Wirral Skip Felagr)

Fig. 11. A modern re-enactor depicting an English warrior of some status in the early tenth century. (Richard Cutts. Model: Dave Capener of Wirral Skip Felagr)

Fig. 12. A modern re-enactor wearing the kit of a less wealthy warrior in the early tenth century: a man who could be fighting on either side. (Richard Cutts. Model: Steve Banks of Wirral Skip Felagr)

Fig. 13. According to an inscription, this small copy of the Psalms, likely made in Reims, was given to King Athelstan by Winchester Cathedral. Included in its pages is this magnificent image of Christ in Majesty. (Album / British Library / Alamy Stock Photo)

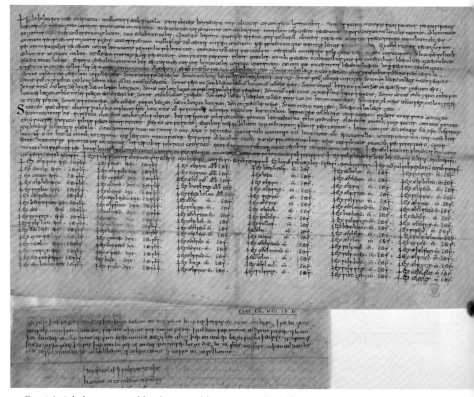

Fig. 14. Athelstan granted lands to a nobleman named Wulfgar in this charter issued from Lifton, Devon, on 12 November 931. Following the king in the witness list are the archbishops of Canterbury and York, followed by Hywel Dda and Idwal Foel, who are recorded as 'sub-kings' from Wales. (© British Library Board. All Rights Reserved / Bridgeman Images)

Fig. 15. The Overchurch Runestone, found during the demolition of its namesake church near Upton, is likely a quarter of what was a larger monumental grave slab created in the ninth century. The inscription reads 'The people erected a memorial ... Pray for Aethelmund'. Today the stone is held by the Grosvenor Museum. (Williamson Art Gallery & Museum, Birkenhead; Wirral Museums Service)

Fig. 16. John Speed's 1611 map of the Wirral, showing *Brunburgh* on the eastern shore. Note also the extension of the sea at Wallasey Pool at upper right, effectively separating Wallasey from the peninsula. (Stanford University Libraries, CC0 1.0)

Fig. 17. A painting by Charles Arthur Cox (*fl.* 1875–1930) showing model boats upon Wallasey Pool, with the spire of St Hilary's rising in the background. The view appears to be from the vicinity of Bidston. (Williamson Art Gallery & Museum, Birkenhead; Wirral Museums Service)

Fig. 18. The remains of Skuldelev 1, a Viking warship now on display at the Roskilde Vikingeskibshallen. (DEA / G. DAGLI ORTI / Getty Images)

Fig. 19. This eighth-century helm, which was unearthed near Coppergate in York, may have belonged to a member of the Northumbrian royal dynasty. (York Museums Trust, CC BY-SA 4.0)

Fig. 20. Photo taken on Rest Hill Road in July 2011, following the publication of the *Brunanburh Casebook*, with the proposed battleground spreading out behind the author's shining head. (The author begs the reader's forgiveness for ever thinking this shirt looked good.) (Michael Livingston)

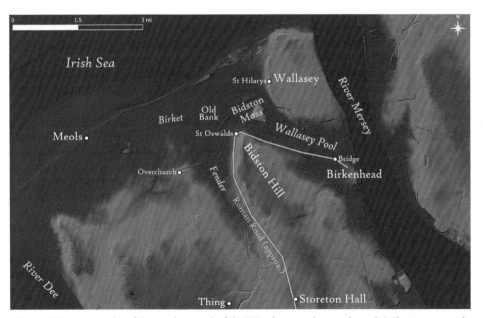

Fig. 21. The topography of the northern end of the Wirral peninsula seen through Lidar imagery and overlaid with key features and a possible route for the Roman road. (Michael Livingston)

Fig. 22. Old Bank today, at the confluence of the Fender and Birket. In his 1922 study of the 'Wirral Watersheds', Eric Rideout reports local rumours that 'skulls, etc.' were found here. (Brian Griffiths)

Fig. 23. The suspected Roman road extends from the middle of the image, heading north up Keepers Lane through Storeton. The area pictured was likely immediately behind Anlaf's lines in 937. (Pete Holder)

Fig. 24. Looking west towards the Dee, the thick trees in the mid-ground mark Brimstage Hall. The Roman road would have passed through the green fields of the foreground from left to right, with the ford over the Brimstage perhaps near the left frame. Storeton rises out of frame to the right (north). (Pete Holder)

Fig. 25. The view over the battlefield, looking north toward the high ground in the middle distance. The Clatterbrook flows in the valley at the right frame, with Red Hill just out of view to the right. Anlaf's lines would have lined up on both sides of the higher ground where the motorway now cuts through the landscape. (Pete Holder)

Fig. 26. The Clatterbrook today, as it flows near Clatterbridge Hospital. This waterway may have defined the east side of the battlefield in 937. (Brian Griffiths)

Fig. 27. Looking south down the zig-zagging line of the Clatterbrook today, with Clatterbridge Hospital in the middle distance. The line of trees along the ridgeline at the upper right may approximate the tree line in 937 and the rough western border of the battlefield. (Pete Holder)

Fig. 28. The battleground as the English may have seen it: looking north towards the ridgeline at Storeton. (Dave Capener)

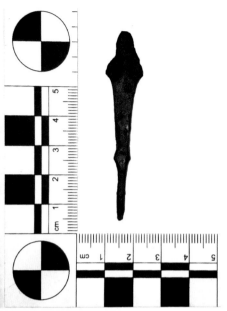

Fig. 29. WA2415, a Scandinavian arrowhead recovered by Wirral Archaeology. (Paul Sherman)

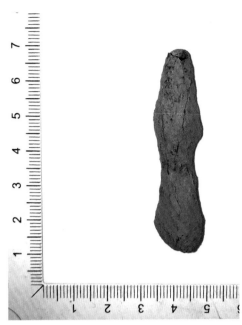

Fig. 30. WA42, a badly corroded arrowhead recovered by Wirral Archaeology. (Paul Sherman)

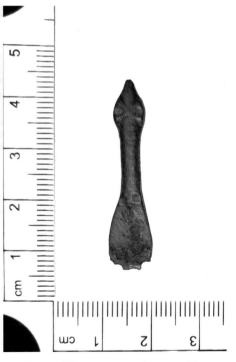

Fig. 31. WA21, a strap end recovered by Wirral Archaeology. (Paul Sherman)

Fig. 32. Gaming pieces recovered by Wirral Archaeology. (Paul Sherman)

Fig. 33. The obverse of a silver penny now held by the York Museums Trust. It reads 'Eþelstan Rex To. Bri.' (Athelstan, king of all Britain). (York Museums Trust, CC BY-SA 4.0)

Fig. 34. The effigy of Athelstan atop his 15th-century monumental tomb in Malmesbury Abbey. (Photo by Geography Photos/Universal Images Group via Getty Images)

STRENGTH AND WEAKNESS

With Eamont concluded and Guthfrith turned back to Ireland, Athelstan shifted his eyes to the west. Within months, he had summoned the Welsh princes to Hereford, where the sources tell us he received *their* submission as well. While we should be sceptical of this event, too, we at least are on firmer ground here. There are references to an enormous tribute being paid to the English at the time, and over the coming years several Welsh leaders would be found in Athelstan's court, witnessing charters under his direction. William also records that Athelstan marched his army into Cornwall, pushing back *that* border, too.[8]

Though we should be wary of giving Athelstan more glory than he deserves with these various submissions, there is no doubting Athelstan's strength after 927. He had, in short order, greatly expanded and secured his territories. His England stretched further north than his grandfather might ever have imagined.

A sense of the exultation within Athelstan's circle can be gleaned from a poem, likely written from York in the days before the king left for Eamont. The poet, who names himself Peter,[9] sends word back to the queen and prince about an England now 'made whole':

King Athelstan lives
glorious through his deeds!

He, with Sihtric having died,
in such circumstances arms for battle
the army of the English
throughout all Britain.

Constantine, king of the Scots,
hastens to Britain:
by supporting the king of the English
[he is] loyal in his service.[10]

For these poets, and for the king himself, Athelstan's seizure of York clearly signified a new status for the crown. It was, quite specifically now, an *English* crown. In a way that no one before him could claim, Athelstan was king of all the English.

Despite his stunning successes, it appears that there were still some even among the English who opposed Athelstan's right to be king. William of Malmesbury informs us that around this time a man named Alfred – a common enough name – led a conspiracy to seize the king in Winchester and blind him. The conspirators were caught, however, and Alfred died in Rome while trying to clear his name with the Pope. This Winchester affair may have occurred as early as 924 and signalled part of the resistance that delayed Athelstan's coronation. Alternatively, it could have occurred as late as 933, when Athelstan's half-brother Edwin (the dead Aelfweard's younger brother) drowned at sea when his ship foundered. Edwin would probably have been made king if Athelstan had been unable to rule, and William tells us that there were old songs connecting the two events: rumours had swirled that Edwin was behind the conspiracy, and Athelstan had exiled him as a result. Edwin was buried in Flanders at the abbey of Saint-Bertin. Edwin's death is confirmed by an account of the abbey's own history, written in 962 by a monk named Folcuin, but the monk doesn't reference his rumoured betrayal.

INVADING SCOTLAND

If there *was* a lingering internal opposition to Athelstan's rule in the early 930s, it might help explain his sudden decision to attack Scotland in 934. Some scholars suggest that the removal of Edwin left Athelstan at last free to attempt a long-desired assault, but this seems to me unlikely: Athelstan had been more than happy to march north to York in 927, when his throne was far less secure. If there is a connection to Edwin, it seems more probable that it reflects a sad but time-proven truth: a foreign war can create domestic peace.

There are other potential explanations. If Constantine II had truly submitted to Athelstan at Eamont Bridge in 927, then there was no reason for Athelstan to attack Scotland. Something had surely happened.

We can only speculate what it was. The *Annals of Clonmacnoise* claims that in 934 Ealdred of Bamburgh died. Likewise, the *Annals of Ulster* tells us that Guthfrith, 'a most cruel king of the Norsemen',[11] died in the same year. It could be that Constantine had attempted to take advantage of the resulting chaos in the north to move in on leaderless territory. If he did, Athelstan might have felt this was a direct threat to his own position in the north, breaking the bonds made at Eamont. Alternatively, the English king could have been the aggressor, seeing the deaths of the rival leaders as one more opportunity to absorb rival lands. It had worked with Sihtric's York, so maybe he tried it with Bamburgh, too.

Whatever the reason, Athelstan headed north. His army marched by land, following Dere Street, while his navy paralleled his track off-shore, not just providing logistical assistance to the campaign but also protecting it from any chance of counter-attack by sea. It was a well-coordinated advance – and a rapid one. On 28 May Athelstan was in Winchester. By 7 June he was already in Nottingham, on his way to Scotland. He stopped at Chester-le-Street to visit the shrine of St Cuthbert (an act of devotion that was also surely calculated to win ecclesiastical support for his crown and his campaign). How far his army marched into Scotland is frustratingly unclear. The *Annals of Clonmacnoise* says he reached Edinburgh before he was turned back by the Scots. A 12th-century compilation of earlier sources, called the *History of the Kings*, including material from at least one otherwise lost northern chronicle, states instead that Athelstan's army marched as far as Dunnottar Castle near Stonehaven and the mountains of Fortriu, while his navy ravaged up the Scottish coastline as far as Caithness. If his ships indeed reached so far, it would have been a provocatory threat against the Viking-held Orkney Islands.

Athelstan was back in England by 13 September, when he signed a charter in Buckingham. With him in court, humbled as a 'sub-king' to Athelstan, was Constantine, which strongly suggests that the longer, more victorious English campaign is the correct one. If so, Athelstan's army had marched from Chester-le-Street to Stonehaven and then back to Buckingham – at least 700 miles – in less than three months. The fact that Owain of Strathclyde likewise appears in the English court as a 'sub-king' suggests that the army's march might also have swung into his territories on the way to or from Scotland, adding still more miles. The English navy had probably sailed hundreds of miles further.

That Athelstan had pulled it all off, apparently without major loss, was an enormous testament to his ability as a leader to organize and inspire his men.

These qualities would be tested again soon enough – and with immeasurably higher stakes. Brunanburh was just three years away.

Athelstan's invasion of Scotland may well have made it inevitable.

6

The Great Alliance, 934–37

For decades, it must have seemed that every year brought greater glory to the English. Athelstan's military fame was spreading well beyond English shores. So, too, was his religious fame: as he had at Chester-le-Street on his way north, he continued to lavish gifts on the Church – possibly driven by his personal devotion, but also showing his shrewd awareness of the Church's potential as a political tool.

Not everyone was happy with Athelstan's rise. Time and again the king had thwarted and embarrassed the other powers in the British Isles. He had taken York from Guthfrith and the Vikings. He had ravaged Constantine's Scotland, and humbled both him and Owain of Strathclyde. He had forced the Welsh kings to pay tribute. He had made them *all*, sometimes more than once, acknowledge his superiority.

These rival kingdoms had no love for each other. The Welsh had fought off the Vikings led by Ingimund. Constantine had spent much of his life killing Vikings. But year by year it had become clearer who the greater threat was.

Alone, no one could stand up to Athelstan.

Together, maybe they could.

It was in this spirit that an unnamed Welshman wrote a poem called *Armes Prydein Vawr*, the *Great Prophecy of Britain*. It's a remarkable tour-de-force of imagery, calling for warriors to scatter their enemies in battle:

> They will bring about rejoicing after devastation
> and reconciliation of the Cymry [i.e. the Welsh] and the men of Dublin.
> The Irish of Ireland, Anglesey, and Scotland,
> the Cornish and the men of Strathclyde will be welcomed among us.
> The Britons will rise again when they prevail.
> Long was prophesied the time when they will come,
> rulers by right of descent taking their possession,
> men of the North in a place of honour around them;
> in the centre of their van they will advance.[1]

The target of this Irish Sea-spanning alliance, the poet goes on to make clear, is the English, who have levied heavy taxes on the Welsh. These foreigners, he says, 'will be driven into exile', landless, without harbour. Hearkening back to the stories of Hengist and Horsa and the coming of the Anglo-Saxons centuries earlier, the poet calls the English 'the shitheads of Thanet', the occupiers of native Briton land.[2]

> The Cymry and Saxons will meet
> upon a bank to destroy and attack one another
> with huge armies when they contend with one another.
> And on a hill – blades and battle-cry and thrusting,
> and on the Wye – shout against shout upon the shining water,
> and dropping of banners, fierce attacking,
> and Saxons will fall as food for wild beasts.
> The followers of the Cymry will line up as one,
> front to rear the palecheeks would be constrained.
> The agents, as payment for their deceit, will wallow in their blood,
> their army in a flood of blood around them.

Others on foot will retreat through the wood.
Through the ramparts of the fortification the 'foxes' will flee.
War will not return to the land of Britain.
Through wretched counsel, they will slip back again like the sea.[3]

He concludes that the English, 'the tormentors of the island', will pass away like 'a swarm of bees', so thoroughly packed in and destroyed that their dead wouldn't have space to fall.[4]

The idea of an anti-English alliance between these many traditional enemies was quite clearly in the air. It was only a matter of time until someone put it into action.

The real question was who it would be. And from where?

* * *

Many in Wales were ready and willing to take the fight to the English, but they weren't unified. In 937 there were probably at least six men in Wales who called themselves king. The most powerful of these were Hywel Dda in Deheubarth, Idwal Foel in Gwynedd, and Llywelyn ab Merfyn in Powys. But there were others: Morgan Hen was in Gwent, his brother Cadwgan in Glywysing, and Tewdwr ap Elisse might have been in Brycheiniog. By around 942, Hywel Dda would have control of all but Glywysing and Gwent, with those two regions united under the rule of Morgan Hen.

That there were so many kingdoms in 937, and that they would so soon be reduced to only a pair, underscores the challenge anyone in Wales would have had in taking the lead against the English. Worse, Hywel Dda, the strongest ruler, appears to have been happy to use the English to help him pursue his own political ends in Wales. Of all the Welsh kings, he was the most friendly to Athelstan.

In the end, it wasn't just that the Welsh kings didn't lead the fight against the English. Not one of the Welsh kings even participated in the grand alliance that would soon set off on a campaign to oppose the English king.

* * *

It's tragic that so few sources can tell us what was happening in the kingdom of Strathclyde, where Owain was king. We think his father had been named Dyfnwal, and we think he had been ruling as king for a few years now. For a brief moment in 937, we're on firmer ground: we know that Owain accompanied King Constantine II of Scotland and King Anlaf of Dublin to Brunanburh.

After that we move quickly into murky speculation, and the fact that we come up empty about so much of his biography makes him an unlikely orchestrator for this grand alliance: having ultimate leadership of the coalition would have been a hard thing to keep secret, and no source gives him any higher position than merely participating in the campaign.

* * *

We've already seen a great deal of Constantine, the now-grey-haired king who had ruled Scotland since 900. He was an experienced and capable leader, so it's tempting to view him as the master organizer who brought everyone to the table and set the plan in motion. He was the most senior man both in physical age and in power. He also had the biggest bone to pick with the English. Athelstan had cut his country deep in 934. Farms were laid waste. Villages were devastated. He had been taken to the English court and paraded out as sub-king to Athelstan, a humiliation of the power and authority of the Scots. If Constantine called his people to arms against the arrogant southerners who had invaded their lands, many would have flocked to his raised banners of war. So the old king had, a police detective might say, the means, the motive, and the opportunity to be the instigating party for a grand anti-English alliance.

But it wasn't him. The famed *Battle of Brunanburh* poem notes Constantine's participation – including the death of his son – alongside the allied kings, but other early sources highlight the Vikings as the primary foe: Symeon of Durham (writing between 1104 and 1115), for instance, says the Viking leader 'had with him the help of the kings of the Scots and Cumbrians (i.e., Strathclyde)', which implies the Vikings were the coordinators of the campaign.[5]

Neither Ælfric of Eynsham in 998 nor the 'F' text of the *Anglo-Saxon Chronicle* (around 1100) even mentions the Scots: the Vikings alone are the enemy.[6] A Scots-led campaign does appear in *Egil's Saga* (between 1220 and 1240), but this is enormously complicated by the fact that it names the 'king of the Scots' Anlaf instead of Constantine.[7] Anlaf is the name of the *Viking* leader. Accounts of the battle specifically recording *Constantine* as the alliance leader only appear much later, probably reflecting a post-Conquest focus on Anglo-Scottish relations.

* * *

According to the *Annals of Clonmacnoise*, Guthfrith had placed his own sons in charge of Dublin when he sailed to make his claim on York in 927. This decision had infuriated the sons of Sihtric, who had thought rule of the city should be theirs now that Guthfrith would take their father's place in Northumbria. They had allied themselves with the Vikings of Limerick and conquered Dublin ... only to be driven back out of the city when Guthfrith returned empty-handed from his attempt to take Northumbria. This set off a period of conflict between these rival groups of Vikings.

Guthfrith's death in 934 didn't end the strife. His son, Anlaf Guthfrithson, succeeded to his father's position in Dublin – and also to his antagonism to the Limerick Vikings. Just three years later, Anlaf settled matters in Ireland and was able to turn towards the resolution of another family grudge: the English grip over lands he thought were rightly his.

Exactly how things ended between the Limerick Vikings and Anlaf's Dubliners is – like so much else in our story so far – not clear. The *Annals of the Four Masters* reports that in 937 Anlaf journeyed from Dublin to Lough Ree. There he and his men attacked the Limerick Vikings, who were led by a man named Olaf Cenncairech. Olaf's ships were broken, and Olaf was taken back to Dublin as a prisoner. This speaks to a decisive battle between these long-antagonistic Viking groups, only weeks after which the king of Limerick travelled with Anlaf to England for the campaign that would lead to Brunanburh.

The *Annals of Clonmacnoise* doesn't even hint at such a battle: it simply says that the Vikings of Limerick came from Lough Ree to Dublin and joined Anlaf in traveling to England. The *Chronicle of Scotland* has a similar bare statement of their coming to Dublin. This indicates that what happened at Lough Ree wasn't a great battle but rather a negotiation and maybe an alliance. Perhaps Olaf agreed to join Anlaf in a mission to beat Athelstan and set things right for both their families – after all, if Anlaf fulfilled his family's claims in England, Olaf might be in a position to fulfil his family's claim on Dublin. As the Welsh *Prophecy* suggested so many of these groups should do, the two men might have set aside what set them apart in favour of what brought them together: their hatred of the English king.

Whatever happened on Lough Ree took place in August. Perhaps eight weeks later, both Anlaf and Olaf were across the sea on the field of Brunanburh. A great deal of work and movement must be packed into those two months to make this possible, including coordination with the other elements of the coalition in Scotland and Strathclyde. Our sources, as we've seen, point to Anlaf as the leader of the great alliance that would come to the field of Brunanburh: so once he had hatched the plan, his messengers would need to go back and forth between Dublin and the overseas kingdoms. Agreements had to be struck. Deals had to be made. Plans – *complex* plans given that three armies needed to unite and do their best to surprise the enemy – had to be devised. Then, once everything was set, logistics needed to be managed: the men of Anlaf's Viking army would need to be gathered, along with the food, weapons, and other supplies they would require for an extended stay on the field. They would also need a great many ships to carry all these provisions and men across the sea. The ships would need to be loaded – its own logistical nightmare given the hundreds of crafts involved and the limited capabilities of even a large medieval harbour like Dublin – before the crossing itself was begun, followed by the sea-journey that would keep the large fleet together while getting it into contact with the allied forces ... who had their own long list of preparations to make. Then there would be the time spent on whatever actual campaign there was *before* Athelstan responded and everyone could come together for the battle itself.

Medieval armies don't appear out of thin air. These weren't standing, ready forces. They needed time to get going, and adding in the naval element and the multi-force coordination only makes things that much more complex, that much more time-consuming.

If the voyage wasn't far, *if* the agreements were made quickly, *if* everything went just right, then it *might* be conceivable that all this could happen in just eight weeks. It would be remarkable, yes, but it would be at least *conceivable*.

It all makes a *great* deal more sense, though, if we push the agreements and the start of campaign planning to an earlier date, perhaps as far back as the spring. Do that, and there's plenty of time for the organization and the impressive execution of the whole endeavour.

Which brings us back to the Vikings of Limerick. Why would Anlaf march off to fight them on Lough Ree when he was in the middle of preparing for a massive invasion of England? Battles are unpredictable, and anything less than complete and total victory would directly weaken his force at the very moment that he most needed to strengthen it. If Lough Ree was a battle, then it seems highly unlikely that planning for the invasion of England could have started until after it – which puts that eight-week timeline even *further* into jeopardy since we would also need to add the time it took him to get back to Dublin.

On the other hand, a journey to Lough Ree to convince another powerful group of Vikings to join a campaign already underway makes perfect sense. The report of ship-breaking and prisoner-taking in the *Annals of the Four Masters* might simply be in error, either the result of confusion on the part of its editors or a fault in the materials they were using: the 'four masters' who composed the *Annals* – using materials now lost – were four men working in a cottage on the grounds of Donegal Abbey between 1632 and 1636. While the dearth of our sources means that even something as full of questions as this needs to be examined, it isn't reasonable to conclude that this witness alone recorded a momentous battle between Limerick and Dublin that the other, more contemporary sources ignored – a battle that also greatly complicates the timeline for the Brunanburh campaign.

* * *

One way or another, after all the deals were done, the alliance was formed. Exactly where and how they came together on the field – where and how Brunanburh was fought – is the question to which we must now turn.

7

Reconstructing Battles

To this point I've referenced a great number of battles ... while describing none of them in detail. What was it like at Ethandun? How did Alfred arrange his men? What tactical decisions did he make? What was it like for the men facing each other, fighting for their lives? What did they see, hear, smell? How did it *feel* to fight in the tenth century?

I have largely avoided such details because they simply don't exist in the ways we would like. It's important to understand why this is, and what it means for our ability to reconstruct battles like Brunanburh.

FACES OF BATTLE

People in battle make decisions based on training and instinct. Often (but not always) these are competing impulses: the instinct for survival may say to retreat; the training for battle may say to push forward. For all else that military hierarchies can accomplish, their most essential function is to corral independent choices, to transform individual fighters into a cohesive army. Cohesion may be driven by the threat of punishment, the promise of glory, the prospect of riches, the protection of loved ones, or even the idea that survival is more likely inside the group than outside it. One way or another the individual must be fused into the collective. The shield-wall provides a perfect example for why this must be so: individuals acting of their own accord will create a gap in the wall, and a gap will get everyone, the brave and the cowardly alike, killed.

The collective nature of armies greatly simplifies the historian's work of understanding human conflict. The fight for Little Round Top on 2 July 1863, for example, was a key moment in the battle of Gettysburg. Colonel Joshua Lawrence Chamberlain, realizing that his position at the far left of the Union line was about to crumble, ordered his men – most of them out of ammunition – to fix bayonets and charge their Confederate attackers. It was an extraordinary action that would earn Chamberlain the Medal of Honor, and no story of Gettysburg can be told without taking account of what the little blue rectangle at the end of the Union line – Chamberlain's 20th Maine Volunteer Infantry Regiment – did that day. The little blue block had been bent back against the Union line, distorted as Chamberlain struggled to hold the flank. But with the charge it straightened out and swung down from its position like a crashing gate, sweeping away the Confederate threat and heroically holding the Union flank.

But the 20th Maine Volunteer Infantry Regiment wasn't a blue rectangle. It was 385 men, who made 385 individual decisions from the moment they were buckling under the Confederate onslaught, firing their last shot into the enemy, to the moment they were fixing bayonets, preparing to charge headlong into the advancing enemy front. It's easier for us to think of the 20th Maine as a blue block, but the truth of that day was quite literally personal. And erasing that individual reality is to make a lie, however well-intentioned, of the truth experienced by the men who fought and died in that perilous moment.

At the same time, a blocks-on-a-map view of warfare is often necessary. Comprehending the 385 individual threads that make up the Union side of the picture of Little Round Top would be hard enough. Placing them within the context of the 175,000 threads of the men around them fighting at Gettysburg? Impossible.

Unfortunately, we don't always have the individual stories. The eyewitness, personal perspective of battle is rare, especially as we move further and further into the past. More often than not we have tragically limited information about the engagements we are studying. Blocks on a map are sometimes the only choice.

Even worse, sometimes we have neither the blocks nor the map.

The great majority of the battles of the Middle Ages survive as little more than a few lines of text: what the battle was called, maybe the names of some of the leaders involved, perhaps a rough scale of army sizes that may fall apart under scrutiny. Even in those instances when we *do* have more information – as we do with Brunanburh – we must proceed with caution.

SOURCES, AGAIN

The problem comes from the nature of our sources. In a 1961 lecture, historian E.H. Carr put it this way:

> No document can tell us more than what the author of the document thought – what he thought had happened, what he thought ought to happen or would happen, or perhaps only what he wanted others to think he thought, or even only what he himself thought he thought.[1]

The ramifications of this are enormous, and they get even worse when we begin to think about how Carr's hypothetical author (and indeed Carr himself) would also be limited in what he *could* think about what he thought. Our educations, our experiences, our language, and many other factors all serve to constrain our thoughts and our ability to communicate them.

To show how these problems unfold, how they make the reality of warfare so difficult to recover, let's start with the battle of Sherston in 1016. What follows is a translation of the account of the battle left to us by a monk named John of Worcester, highlighting the actions of Edmund Ironside, who was king of England from 23 April to 30 November of that year:

> When he arranged the army according to the location and his forces, he drew the best into the front line, he arranged the

remainder of the army in reserve, and calling each man by name, exhorted and requested that they remember that they fought for country, children, wives and for homes, and with these rousing words he fired the soldiers' hearts; thereafter he ordered the trumpeters to sound and the cohorts to gradually advance. The enemy army did the same. When they had come to where they could join battle they rushed forward with great clamour and with hostile standards. The battle was borne with lances and swords, with all their might it was fought. Meanwhile King Edmund Ironside took a position in fierce hand-to-hand fighting in the front rank; he perceived of everything. He himself fought hard, he often struck the enemy; he performed at the same time the duties of a tough soldier and a good general.[2]

At first glance, this would be an enormously valuable source for anyone wishing to reconstruct what happened at Sherston. Details about troop dispositions and movements might give us blocks on a map, and some folks have used this passage to create just that. Yet scholars have revealed that the account is almost entirely lifted from Sallust's *Wars with Catiline*, detailing the battle of Pistoia in 62 BC.[3] So the only hope for extracting *any* actual tactical information about Ironside's actions from John of Worcester's account would be to assume, first, that the monk – writing 50 miles and more than 100 years away from the events at Sherston – inexplicably knew the truth of what happened there; second, that he decided to work through the classical sources he knew looking for an exact match to these actions; third, that the actions at Sherston somehow really *did* match those over a thousand years earlier at Pistoia; and, fourth, that when John recognized this remarkable coincidence he decided to use Sallust's words rather than his own.

This is an almost impossible chain of assumptions. It's doubtful that John of Worcester knew anything unique about Sherston, and it's exceedingly unlikely that whatever really happened there – even *if* John knew about it and understood it – was a perfect tactical match to a millennium-old battle in Italy. To the contrary, John's use of Sallust is likely the result of his desire to spice up his work and perhaps show off, to anyone who recognized the plagiarism, how well he knew his Sallust. It's near useless as history.

Fair enough. Forget John of Worcester, you might say. Let's set him aside and find someone who doesn't borrow from other sources as he does, and instead gives us original facts.

The easiest way to find such an 'original' voice would be to use a computer to search sets of words from a potential source against the words in a database of other sources, looking for common strings of words. But what does it really tell us if such a search comes up clean? It tells us simply that our text doesn't match anything in our database ... a database that we know doesn't include all possible texts. We have already seen that William of Malmesbury had access to materials now lost when he was writing his book. And the further back in time we go, the greater the number of lost texts becomes.

I've picked on John of Worcester here mostly because he's an easy target – it's not the only time he pulls this sort of stunt – but we have to worry about source reliability when we're looking at *any* battle. Are we being told the truth? How would we even know?

OUR RECONSTRUCTION TOOLKIT

Conflict analysis is a fancy term for what we're about to do: locate and reconstruct a battle. Like any specialist endeavour, it uses a specific set of tools, but the tools aren't the job. Having a hammer doesn't make you a carpenter. And while experienced carpenters might hang certain tools on their belts most of the time, they won't hesitate to swap them out if the job necessitates it. You use the tools you need.

Of all the tools in the conflict analyst's kit, perhaps the easiest to understand is archaeology. If our sources say that something happened, it locks things down quite neatly if archaeologists can also dig up the evidence of exactly that something happening. On the flip side, if our sources say something happened – the laying waste of Britain when the so-called Anglo-Saxons arrived, for instance – it's problematic if archaeologists can't find any compelling evidence of it. It may mean that our sources aren't quite telling the truth.

(*Maybe*, because it could be that the *next* shovel in the dirt will find the evidence that we thought wasn't there!) Because archaeology can produce verifiable physical evidence of what happened, it is an indispensable tool when it comes to any historical investigation, but in conflict analysis it can be an absolute god-send: as we will see, a battle is its ground, and archaeology is one of the only ways to confirm the ground upon which a battle was fought.

Yet there are several weaknesses with archaeology. The first is that there must be something to dig up. Some events leave no mark upon the landscape, no remains to be unearthed. Other events have been built over: streets and buildings are perched atop priceless evidence that's now forever hidden from view. A second weakness is that archaeology requires a commitment of time and resources that our buzzing world often doesn't have the patience for. We want answers now, and we want them as cheap as we can get them. A third problem is that archaeology is destructive. We may use our finest tools and expert analysis as we sift through the earth, but such is the inevitable advancement of science and technology that we could be throwing away dirt that contains valuable information we don't yet know how to access. (How much more would we have been able to glean about the tomb of King Tut if it was opened today rather than in 1922!) Still, archaeology can provide the closest thing to a 'smoking gun' when it comes to the past.

Another great tool we have when it comes to proving or disproving our sources is what I call 'multi-source verification': we compare multiple sources for an event, and if they agree then we have more reason to trust the story we're being told. It doesn't mean we *know* that the information is true, though. It could be that our multiple sources ultimately derive from a single and inaccurate report of the event. It could be that they are all written under the sway of the same social or political influence. Still, in a game of probabilities we will take any relative advantage we can get. Betting everything on a single source is too often akin to trusting a random blog to give you the straight dope on a contentious political issue. You are completely vulnerable to the blogger's agenda, their biases, and above all their mistakes.

Multi-source verification requires multiple sources – and we're often lucky to have a single one. So it's vital to cast as wide a net as possible when it comes to what we consider sources. Most folks seeking sources for a medieval battle will think about the traditional chronicle accounts. But what about tax records, charters, royal writs, parish records, and all the other documents that might obliquely reference the event? A single person seeing ripples strike the edge of a pond may know relatively little. But the timing and strength of those ripples, seen from three separate points around the shore, allows one to reconstruct when and where a rock hit the water – and even get a sense of how big it was. The impact of human conflict is the same: it spreads across society and leaves its mark in ways large and small. The more sources we can find – no matter how small they might be – the better chance we have of triangulating the event behind them.

Another basic tool of conflict analysis is our ever-evolving knowledge of warfare. Based on what we have learned from other battles, how do we think men typically fought in this period? Could their ranged weapons have shot far enough to accomplish what they're said to have accomplished? How were they trained to respond to situations? Most of these questions and answers will be highly specific and unique to an engagement.

In addition to all this, there are some basic principles that I keep in my personal toolbox when approaching a battle. They aren't so universally true that they can be called 'rules', but they're common enough that they can provide some basic guidelines about how men behave in combat – a useful set of maxims when trying to reconstruct events.

Follow the roads. Before a battle can take place, armies have to get to the field. That means the large-scale movement of men and their goods across landscapes that, in their natural form, do not facilitate that transport. Thousands of men. Hundreds of wagons. Perhaps herds of animals for food supply. And all of them needing to be moved as quickly as possible. Efficient logistics may not make for an exciting scene in a movie, but the goal of a campaign, perhaps the fate of a nation, very often depends upon the speed of transport. That means that the armies involved, if at all possible, will travel on roads. As a result, battles are most likely to fall on or close to roads.

No man is a fool. This maxim encapsulates two basic ideas for me. First, everyone in the battle-line feels the imminence of death. They know the danger. They know the fear. They aren't fools. So they need a reason to follow, a reason to fight. Knowing what they were fighting for can, at times, help us surmise where their battle-lines were run. Second, leaders will make the best decision they can with the information they have. It may be that a tactical decision appears incredibly wrong in retrospect – 'What the hell were those idiots thinking?' is a common refrain among battlefield tourists – but one shouldn't assume the leaders to be fools. Odds are, they were thinking *something.* They had, in the moment of action, a sense of purpose. It may be that they had a fatal limitation in their field-awareness. It may be that they had a false sense of security in their armaments or their experience, or they were blinded by their egos. Getting to the heart of why a miscalculation occurred does far more for the conflict analyst than dismissing one side or the other as fools.

A battle is its ground. Ground is critical in a combat not just because the ideal positioning of a small force on highly favourable terrain can overcome massive numerical or even technological disadvantages. Even before the fighting unfolds, ground also determines the lines of sight available to the commanders taking position. It determines how and where their men can be brought to bear upon the enemy. It determines the lines of approach they must take. It determines the speed at which they can move. It can even determine whether they ride or walk, how much armour they can wear, or which weapons they can carry. A proper reconstruction of a battle must therefore consider the largest picture of the ground possible. Not just its basic topography, but the historical geology and hydrology that has shaped it. Studying a battle without studying its ground is like buying a car without taking it for a test-drive. You know what you think will happen when you try to make it go, but the truth is you have no idea if it will work. Maybe you lucked out and everything is in working order. But just as likely, maybe even more likely, you bought a dud sitting on blocks.

Men move like water. Water follows the path of least resistance, and so will men in battle. This doesn't mean that men will necessary flow downhill – though very often they will – but that because they aren't fools their movements will largely be determined by what they perceive to be the path of least resistance. Just as roads were the easiest possible route for them to reach the battlefield, so, too, will there be routes easy and hard when it comes to their movement across or away from that ground.

There are more tools that the conflict analyst can bring to bear. But this should be enough of a kit for us to begin the work of not just finding Brunanburh, but ultimately reconstructing it.

8

The Search for Brunanburh

It's no surprise that the site of the battle of Brunanburh has been lost. After the field was picked over by men and beasts, no great monument was erected to mark the place. This was typical. With few exceptions – Battle Abbey at Hastings, for instance, or Battlefield Church at Shrewsbury – there seems to have been a medieval lack of interest in constructing lasting battle memorials.

The veterans of such battles no doubt remembered. They were living memorials. They carried the places they fought, and the terrors they experienced under arms, etched into the fabric of their remaining lives: warfare scars the body, but it just as equally (and more universally) sears the mind.

The St Crispin's Day speech in Shakespeare's *Henry V*, for instance, is often rightly remembered for the king's profession of an immediate shared experience in combat – the 'band of brothers' forged in the fight – but it can just as easily be read for what it says about the battle-trauma that could mark both the body and mind of the fighting man:

He that shall live this day, and see old age,
Will yearly on the vigil feast his neighbours,
And say 'To-morrow is Saint Crispian'.
Then will he strip his sleeve and show his scars,
And say 'These wounds I had on Crispin's day'.

Old men forget; yet all shall be forgot,
But he'll remember ...[1]

Still, measured against the long line of human history, our lives
are short. So despite the central importance of personal traumas
in the lives of veterans – and in the lives of their loved ones, who
inevitably share the burden – societies contextualize battles against
a wider field. As a result, a battle is more often remembered for
what happened, not *where* it happened.[2] The larger, long-term
significance of conflict is acquired when total costs can be counted,
lasting outcomes can be realized, cultural responses can be matured,
and connections to political goals can be drawn. The last of these is
particularly important to note, as political dynamics can shape not
only *how* but also *if* a battle is remembered by future generations.
At the simplest level, the victories of political foes may be erased,
and their losses magnified, whereas the victories of political friends
may be glorified, and their losses diminished or excused.

Even in cases where it *would* be politically convenient to
remember a battle's location – as it would be for Athelstan and
his immediate successors to the English throne to remember
Brunanburh – the very nature of this kind of conflict can make
it difficult. Unlike sieges, which are generally easy to locate since
they're inherently fixed to the fortified positions under siege, battles
tend to take place in the spaces *between* fixed sites. Just looking
at the most famous battles in English history – Hastings, Crécy,
Agincourt, Waterloo, and, before them all, Brunanburh – it is
evident that they were all fought when armies on the move between
locations encountered other armies on the move between locations.
This between-ness inevitably reduces our fixed-point references,
which in turn greatly increases the difficulty of knowing where and
how these engagements were fought.

One might expect that battlefield locations would nevertheless
be rooted in local memory, but this is often not the case. And even
when local traditions do exist, conflict archaeology is increasingly
showing us they should be judged with some scepticism. The battle
of Bosworth (1461), for instance, holds a central importance in

British history as the field on which King Richard III was killed. As such, there were many local traditions about where it took place. Yet when archaeologists discovered the physical remains of the battle in 2009, they were two miles away from the marvellous new visitor centre that had been built on the location that had been presumed since Victorian times. Similarly, despite the fact that there are traditional sites for Hastings (1066), Crécy (1346), and Agincourt (1415) – with corresponding visitor centres and museums, t-shirts and plaques – there remains a significant probability that the reason we have no archaeological remains from these fields is that we're looking in the wrong places.[3] Happily, none of these are radical shifts in location, mostly due to the fact that the names given to the battles and the records of them that exist provide relatively firm locations from which to triangulate the battle-sites between them.

Brunanburh has proved a much harder case than any of these. The between-ness of Brunanburh isn't marked out by well-travelled, well-known locations. No map, medieval or modern, has a place clearly marked *Brunanburh* on it – much less the other clues our sources give us about the battle. As a result, people have been free to theorize its location almost anywhere in Britain.

And they have. There are dozens of different theories about the location of Brunanburh, ranging from as far in the south as the Severn valley to as far north as southern Scotland, from east to west across the whole of the island. It's easy to understand why there's been such interest: this was a momentous event, one of the most important in the history of the British Isles, yet the relatively sparse information about it means that with enough leaps of faith one could put it almost anywhere.

Brunanburh theorists break down into two general camps. One camp begins with an assumption about the campaign's motivations and builds a theory about the battle accordingly: if the campaign's target was *there*, then Brunanburh must have been around *here*. At first glance, this approach has much to recommend it: a military campaign must have an objective that determines its target and its point of entry to attack said target. The trouble is, no early source tells us the aim or intention of the grand alliance at Brunanburh beyond its being arrayed against the English. It's true that later writers have *assumed* some of these things – filling in blanks, as it were – but it would be quite false to say that we *know* any of them. All we truly know about the Brunanburh campaign is a scattering of place-names.

This brings us to the other camp of theorists, whom the motivation group often derides as 'the place-name people'. Here, one begins with the verifiably certain facts – the place-names in the sources – and tries to connect them with sites on the landscape. Those sites, then, are used to try to ascertain the motivation of the campaign: if Brunanburh was *here*, then the campaign's target must have been *there*.

Each approach is pretty much the opposite of the other, and the camps that they define aren't remotely unified in terms of their results. No matter which path you take, you end up with dozens – perhaps hundreds – of competing theories about its location.

When it comes to Brunanburh, I am, in all transparency, a place-name person. Those few words are the only clues that I can definitively tie to this battle. There may be questions about where those words came from or what they are meant to point us towards, but there can be no questions in the fact that they are there, facing us in 1,000-year-old ink: There was a battle in a place called Brunanburh.

THE NAMES OF BRUNANBURH

Almost any site in England with the letters *B-R-N* in its name has been put forward as a candidate site for *Brunanburh* at one point or another. It's easy to see why. The most prominent element of the battle is indeed that vanished name, which is what it is called in the famous *Anglo-Saxon Chronicle* poem.

But the *Anglo-Saxon Chronicle* isn't the only source that mentions the battle. And not everyone who mentioned it called it *Brunanburh*. In fact, there are at least nine different place-names for the battle:[4]

Place-name	Source	Date	Language	Meaning
Brunanburh	Anglo-Saxon Chronicle	late tenth century	Old English	Fortification of Brune
Brune	Annals of Wales	late tenth century	Welsh	Brune
Brunandune	Aethelweard	c. 980	Old English	Hill of Brune
Wendune	Symeon of Durham	1104–15	Old English	Holy hill
Brunnanwerc	Symeon of Durham	1104–15	Old English	Fortification of Brune
Brunefeld	William of Malmesbury	1127	Old English	Field of Brune
Bruneford	William of Malmesbury	1127	Old English	Ford of Brune
Vinheithr	Egil's Saga	1220–0	Old Norse	Uncultivated meadow
Plaines of Othlyn	Annals of Clonmacnoise	.?1627	Old Irish	?Plains beside the pool

Quite a few of these names are clearly variations on *Brunanburh* – or, indeed, *Brunanburh* may even be a variation on one of them – but several look to be completely independent names for the battle-site. Unhelpfully, not *one* of these options is on maps today. They're all just as mysterious as *Brunanburh*.

This is, itself, a clue. Wherever the battle took place, it can hardly have been well-travelled ground: separate groups gave it separate names, and none of them chose a recognizable location. It cannot have been a well-populated place. More than that, the battle-site must have been at some distance from other, more well-known locations that could have been used to triangulate its position for later readers.

In fact, only one sequence of sources associates the Brunanburh campaign with an identifiable place-name: John of Worcester, a

monk who completed his chronicle featuring the battle in the
1140s, wrote that it occurred near the Humber. His work was
then copied almost verbatim by Symeon of Durham on one of the
two occasions that he wrote about the battle, and it was likewise
repeated by the *Chronicle of Melrose* and the chronicle of Roger of
Howden. All of these writers, quite clearly, had John's text in front
of them. And they all, to judge from their repeating it, believed
what he wrote.

THE FOLLY OF A HUMBER LOCATION

We met John in the previous chapter, when we saw that he
plagiarized his account of the battle of Sherston (a more recent
battle to his time than distant Brunanburh) from Sallust. His
reliability should probably already be in question. But let's set
his plagarism aside for the moment and take what he says about
Brunanburh at face-value:

> Anlaf, the pagan king of the Irish and of many other islands,
> incited by his father-in-law Constantine, king of the Scots,
> entered the mouth of the River Humber with a strong fleet.
> King Athelstan and his brother, Prince Edmund, stood against
> him with an army at the place called Brunanburh.[5]

For what it's worth, no one else claims that Anlaf was married to
Constantine's daughter. We have no idea if it's true. If it is, it would
be a fascinating insight into some of the backstory of the grand
alliance that had come against Athelstan. Perhaps Anlaf had agreed
to the marriage as part of the negotiation? Given John's issues as a
source, I'm doubtful, but it's still interesting to speculate.

The more immediate point of interest, though, is his statement
that Anlaf's fleet sailed into the Humber. Despite the vastness of
the Humber watershed, this would be an important clue. It would
give us a restricted range in which to search for candidate sites.
It would be so absolutely useful, in fact, that it's rather eyebrow-
raising how of all of our Brunanburh sources only John – writing

two centuries after the battle – bothers to mention it. Nevertheless, his claim of a Humber entry is the objection most commonly mustered against the location for Brunanburh that I will present here. So it's important to deal with this up front.

I earlier talked about some of the enormous logistical challenges that each of the three invading armies faced. Anlaf and the Vikings from Ireland had the most difficult task of all. No matter where the battle happened, they had to cross the Irish Sea to get there. These troubles, and the cramped schedule between Lough Ree and Brunanburh, as we saw, make it likely that plans for the campaign were in place before the summer, and that Lough Ree wasn't so much a battle as it was a gathering of strength. There were only so many days in which everything needs to have happened.

That window grows even smaller when we recognize that the English did not have a standing army in place waiting for them. We need time to get the invading armies to England, then to the battle-site, but just as importantly we need time for Athelstan, once aware of the invasion, to gather together his own forces – more and more logistics – before he could ride out to meet the attack. In the shortest timing of things, the battle of Brunanburh could have happened right away after all this, but some of our most detailed sources on the battle add even more days. In *Egil's Saga*, for instance, the invaders waste English lands as messages run back and forth to Athelstan before all parties agree to meet at Brunanburh. Still more time must be added as the forces then gathered there for the battle in which the winner would take all.

It is remarkable that all this could happen in perhaps two months. If we assume planning beginning much earlier in the year, and we place the battle of Brunanburh on western shores – where Anlaf and his army need 'only' cross the Irish Sea – it is just believable.

But what if we place Brunanburh on eastern shores, as John of Worcester suggests?

There are essentially two ways to get from Dublin to the Humber by sea. The southern route through the English Channel is about 870 miles. The northern route around Scotland is about 930 miles. Of the two routes we can surely assume that Anlaf would have taken the northern route. He needed to rendezvous with the Scots, the men of Strathclyde, and potentially other Viking leaders, as well. The direct shot from Dublin to the Wirral is less than 125 miles, whereas arrival at the Humber would mean at least an additional 800 miles of travel across the treacherous late-season sea – greatly increasing chances of shipwreck, separation, interception, ruination by disease, and many other chance factors. Such a long and difficult journey would cause the number and quality of transports needed to rise dramatically. Also increased would be the number of navigational experts required to guide them. There is a vast difference, after all, between a straight shot across the Irish Sea to the Wirral, in which the prevailing winds will more or less send the vessel there by default, and the kind of careful navigation necessary to get an enormous fleet all the way around the British Isles – a difficulty the Spanish Armada learned about in early August 1588.

To cut a long story short, for a Humber campaign the costs in supplies, transports, and men rapidly balloon to the point of absurdity, to say nothing of the increase in time needed to make it all happen. If it is *just* believable that Anlaf could make it from Lough Ree to the west of England in two months, it is simply *not* believable to think he went from Lough Ree to the east of England in the same time span.

One could try to argue that on this single occasion John of Worcester must not mean the same waterway that we mean by the name Humber, but this, too, must surely be discarded: every other time he talks about the Humber he is talking about our Humber.

Most likely, John is simply and completely wrong that the battle happened on the east coast of England and his testimony ought to be viewed accordingly in our search for the site.[6]

So why would John say it happened on the Humber when it didn't?

THE BEVERLEY VISIT

One possibility is that John was confused by a story that Athelstan had visited the shrine of St John of Beverley – which is close to the

Humber – on his way to fight off an invading army from Scotland: this story survives in the work of William Ketel, a 12th-century chronicler who wrote about the miracles associated with St John (d. 721).[7] Ketel was by no means intending to preserve an important sequence of military history, but in talking about one sequence of St John's miracles he may have done just that.

According to Ketel, one year (he doesn't say which) the king of Scotland invaded England by crossing the river that divided their lands. Towns were depopulated, the people killed, the farms ravaged. In his narrative, King Athelstan, marching north in response, meets several people in the region of Lindsey (Lincolnshire today) who had received miracles from St John of Beverley. Moved by their stories, the king sends his army by road towards York while he himself takes a boat across the Humber to visit the saint's shrine at Beverley. With much prayer and devotion, Athelstan places a knife on the altar and is given a church banner to fly before his army. The Scots, hearing of his approach, retreat north, back across the river dividing England from Scotland. Athelstan, reaching that bank himself, receives a vision from the blessed St John telling him to cross the river and invade Scotland, so he does exactly that. Crossing the river and marching north, he puts the lands he conquers under tribute. Near Dunbar, he receives a sign of God's blessing – through St John, of course – when he is able to thrust a sword into a rock. All Scotland quickly falls into English subjugation, and on his return to England, the triumphant king presents his armour and other gifts to the church at Beverley, in thanks for the saint's worldly intercession.[8]

On the whole, the story is a fascinating, if fanciful, tale.

It's also not about Brunanburh. Ketel nowhere mentions that battle or the Vikings or any other alliance leaders. It's an exclusively English–Scottish conflict, and the English campaign that he describes heading north in conquest is very obviously Athelstan's campaign against the Scots which did just that in 934 – even down to the tributary results.

Most later writers who recorded the story knew that the Beverley visit had nothing at all to do with Brunanburh. Like Peter of

Langtoft, who included it in his metrical chronicle around the year 1300, they keep the events entirely separate: one was in 934, the other was in 937.[9] But not everyone could resist the temptation to conflate the two fights against the Scots into a single extraordinary event. *The Chronicle of Crowland*, written around 1400, stitches them into a single piece. And a fair number of Humber theorists do the same thing today when they claim that the Beverley visitation supports John's tale of a Humber entry for Brunanburh. It would be the height of irony, but perhaps John, too, was similarly confused.

ASSUMING MOTIVES

Another option is that John of Worcester, writing in the 1140s, faced the very same problem that the rest of us have. He knew Brunanburh was famous. He knew it was important. But he didn't know where it happened.

In the absence of fact, he assumed.

It was an understandable assumption. Wrong, but essentially understandable. And, interestingly, it's the same understandable-but-wrong assumption that many modern, well-meaning researchers have made when they've decided to trust his account despite the many red flags planted on it. The assumption is that Brunanburh was about York.

True enough, over the chapters of this book we have witnessed decades of conflict over the control over Northumbria, a struggle between the very kingdoms that now stood allied against Athelstan. York-as-motivation is an especially appealing assumption, though, if Brunanburh is viewed with an isolated focus on Anlaf. His father had been denied the throne of York, and later, after Athelstan's death in 939, he himself would indeed march upon and seize that city. Brunanburh, John probably surmised, was simply one more stage of this same long-running dispute.

To that end, the second entry in the *Anglo-Saxon Chronicle* after the famous *Battle of Brunanburh* poem is another, less-famed poem, called the *Capture of the Five Boroughs*. It glorifies the accomplishments of Athelstan's successor, King Edmund, as he reconquered eastern Mercia in 942, just five years after Brunanburh. Mercia, as that poem defines it, is bordered by the Humber. John, assuming that Brunanburh was singularly about control of York and Northumbria, no doubt figured that it would make sense for it to occur on that border, on the Humber. And if Anlaf fled the battle via ship – we're certain that John had the *Anglo-Saxon Chronicle* at hand, and that's exactly what the *Brunanburh* poem says happened – then everything would appear to line up for the theorizing monk: the alliance was trying to get to York by sailing up the Humber, the tributaries of which run up to and, in the case of the Ouse, through the city itself. After all, as John knew, this was the very route that would be taken by Harald Hardrada when he and Tostig Godwinson attacked the city in 1066, just before the battle of Stamford Bridge. In sum, the monk assumed that Anlaf's aim was York, so he assumed that the Humber was the route.

As I've said, many modern historians have followed this very same logic. It seems reasonable. It seems to fit into what comes before and after.

Yet we've already seen the logistical problems with a Humber entry. And now we can add to its problems this: for the two centuries up to John, not one source mentions the Humber or York in relation to *any* part of the campaign that led to the battle. Yet these very same sources name-drop both the river and the city before and after 937 in relation to other events. They knew all too well the centrality of these locations amid the struggles over the north in their time. Aethelweard, the chronicler who wrote of the continuing fame of Brunanburh in his day – it was 'the great battle' – was signing charters for the English king only one year after the last Viking king of York was killed. He would be more than happy to mention York whenever it was the centre of a dispute, so why didn't he do it this time?

A reasonable answer is that he – and everyone else up to John – knew the Brunanburh campaign wasn't aimed at York.

Or, perhaps more accurately said, the campaign wasn't *directly* aimed at York. It's my own assumption – I hope a reasonable one – that Anlaf's own approach to the negotiations for the grand alliance centred on his claims in England. But York was hardly the only bit of English lands that he and his fellow Vikings would have felt they were owed. He could have conceivably desired a restoration to the conditions that had been formally laid out in the Treaty of Alfred and Guthrum: he would have everything north of a line running 'along the Thames, and then along the Lea to its source, then in a straight line to Bedford, and then along the Ouse to Watling Street'. The back and forth of raids and campaigns that his ancestors had been engaged in for the previous 70 years had certainly been fought against the background of that agreement, so why wouldn't Anlaf have thought likewise when it came to this grand alliance against the English? York was in his mind, but it didn't stand alone.

And what about the aims of the two other kings in the alliance? Constantine had personally fought a bloody battle against York-focused Vikings – including Anlaf's father – at Corbridge. Owain had been similarly engaged in dealing with threats from the Irish Sea. Would they truly gain anything from Anlaf seizing York?

The Humber-faithful will answer that yes, they would get a buffer between their lands and those of the belligerent Athelstan. True this may be, but trading one known enemy for another known enemy isn't necessarily the best reason to go to war – no matter how much they might have hated the English at this point. Surely there was something more tangible in the offering. 'Help me get rid of Athelstan', Anlaf must have told them, 'and we can rewrite the maps entirely.'

This is the sort of thing from which alliances between former enemies are made: a greater enemy destroyed and positive gains on all sides. And the most reasonable win-win-win for all three kings would have seen the English pushed back to the Guthrum–Alfred line. Anlaf would hold the former Danelaw, with Olaf of Lough Ree taking over Dublin back in Ireland – the perceived slights to their respective families erased. Constantine's Scotland would extend down the eastern coast, subsuming the former English holdings around Bamburgh maybe as far as the River Tees. Owain's Strathclyde would stretch down the western coast, perhaps as far as the Lake District. Whatever the prior failures of these northern leaders – at Corbridge and Eamont Bridge, for example – the present would be an enormous victory, with a bright new future secured. And the *one* thing standing in the way of these dreams was the *one* person they each had reason to hate: Athelstan.

Re-centre Brunanburh on what could give them all reason to risk their lives – *no man is a fool* – and it's quickly apparent that we cannot blindly assume York as the immediate objective. Again, it's quite understandable that John and the scholars who want to follow him would make that leap. York was definitely part of the mix in 937. But the Brunanburh campaign was something far larger, far more threatening. At Brunanburh, as Eadmer of Canterbury later wrote, Athelstan fought 'an immense army of pagans assembled against the English kingdom'.[10] It wasn't just one more attempt to put York back in Viking hands. It was an alliance of kings whose aim threatened the very existence of Athelstan's realm.

Put it all together, and locating Brunanburh on the east coast of England is right out. We've got to look west.

THE BRUNANBURH CHECKLIST

When we remove John's Humber – as we must – what are we left with? We have the place-names still. Not just *Brunanburh*, but *Wendune* and *Bruneford* and all the rest. Those different names suggest that the location isn't in a well-known or well-populated location. It isn't much, but it's a start. For a checklist, so far, we want a location:

- on the west coast of Britain.
- off the beaten path.

That said, we don't want a location *too* far off the beaten path. Remember the maxim *follow the roads*? As we're narrowing down our search we need to have an eye to how these armies might all have arrived there. Ease of transport will be important.

If we assume that the various names given to the battle reflect what various people remembered of the site, then ideally we want ground that could account for as many of these place-names as possible – not just *Brunanburh*. That would mean a location that could be remembered as being near:

- a low hill with a relatively level summit (the *dun* of both *Brunandune* and *Wendune*).
- a fortified site (the *burh* of *Brunanburh* and the *werc* of *Brunnanwerc*).
- an uncultivated field (the *feld* of *Brunefeld* and the *heithr* of *Vinheithr*).
- an open, flat area (the *vin* of *Vinheithr* and the *plaines* of *Othlyn*).
- a river with a water-crossing (the *ford* of *Bruneford*).
- a local religious site (the *wen* of *Wendune*).

There's some wiggle room in these requirements, because we can't always be 100 per cent sure what these words are meant to represent. Spelling isn't standardized in the Middle Ages – people tended to spell words the way they said them – and the same sound can represent more than one meaning even within the same language. There are still problems with homophones in Modern English today, of course: class going badly because it was a bore is rather different from class going badly because it was a boar – even though these sentences sound the same when spoken aloud. In the case of the various sounds in our place-names, then, it may be that the *vin* of *Vinheithr* is really a mis-remembering of the *wen* of *Wendune*, or vice versa. As with just about everything else we've been dealing with, it comes down to probabilities, and these are what scholars have agreed to be the most probable meanings of these words.[11]

This leaves two main elements to be accounted for in the place-names: *Othlyn* and, most obviously, the *Brun* that features in so many of the forms.

The place-name *plaines of Othlyn* is uniquely recorded in the *Annals of Clonmacnoise*. Though I've referenced this text before, I haven't explained how simultaneously frustrating and tantalizing it is as a source. Working in the castle of Lemanaghan in 1627, historian Conall Mag Eochagáin translated an 'ould Irish book' into 17th-century English. The book he was copying, written in Irish Gaelic, was an annalistic account of the history of Ireland to 1408, and due to its focus on events along the River Shannon it's assumed that it was a product (or a product of products) from the monastery at Clonmacnoise. It's usually named accordingly (as in this book), but in truth we don't know if it's really connected to that monastery or not. We also don't know how old the book really was, though the vast majority of scholars are convinced it preserves very old information. In fact, it's conceivable that its account of Brunanburh, though only about a paragraph in length, is among the earliest extant sources, which would make it very exciting indeed. Yet that 'ould book' Conall was translating from has since vanished.[12] Without the source text to compare his translation to, we can't be certain how much he altered its meaning (intentionally or not) when he translated it. That said, Conall's tortured wording and more-Irish-than-English syntax favours the idea that, as he claimed, he was dutifully preserving what he read. So that's good news, except that *othlyn* isn't a word in either English or Irish. For all his careful work, Conall (or another scribe before him) presumably corrupted a place-name that we would *really* like to know.

The most common theory has been that *othlyn* refers to the Lyme, a geological upland that stretches roughly from the vicinity of Newcastle-under-Lyme to Ashton-under-Lyne.[13] I previously accepted this notion myself, though not without misgivings. It's strange, for instance, that in this one instance the chronicler would identify an important location through such a truly vague place-name. It was, he goes on to say, 'a great slaughter', with numerous leaders fallen among the 34,000 dead on the field (we will return to that number shortly). To say that it happened 'on the plains near the Lyme' would be like identifying the battle of Hastings in 1066 as 'on the hills near the English Channel'. It's possible, yes, but fairly unlikely. Instead, I now think that *othlyn* is a simple mistake – whether by Conall or by the source he was copying. As young scholars in the field quickly learn, the letters *c* and *t* are frightfully easy to confuse for each other in the handwriting common to most medieval Irish manuscripts.

(Both letters were written with the same two strokes as the lower-case *t* in this book's font: only the height of the vertical stroke above the crossbar – which is easy for a scribe to botch – differentiates them.) If this happened to the *Annals of Clonmacnoise* we would have not *othlyn* but *ochlyn*, a very reasonable presentation of an original Old Irish *och-linn*, meaning 'by the pool'. Conall elsewhere interchanges *lyn* and *linn* in exactly this same way: he refers to Dublin as *Dublyn* on multiple occasions, for instance, including in his entry that describes when the sons of Sihtric 'tooke Dublyn' after Guthfrith attempted to claim York in 927.[14] Rather than a general topographical description, though, this was probably a place-name, not unlike the 'black pool' from which Dublin (Old Irish *Duibhlinn*) itself was born. Othlyn, or more properly Ochlin, would have been a harbour settlement by the sea, characterized by a large pool.

The famed *Battle of Brunanburh* poem also points us to a location near a body of water beside the sea. After his defeat in the battle, Anlaf is described as fleeing to the safety of his ships, which launch from a place called *Dingesmere*. The word *mere* is common enough in Old English. It typically means a pool or body of water in the landscape. The other part of the word is more problematic, but there is a strong argument to be made on linguistic grounds that it means 'of the Thing', the assembly place at which Viking societies would gather to establish laws and conduct other matters of community business.[15] *Dingesmere*, then, would mean the pool of the Thing – looking very much like the same pool that may be behind the *Othlyn* of the *Annals of Clonmacnoise*.

We can, from all this, add two more conditions to our ideal battle-site. It should also be:

- near but not at a harbourage for the allied ships (the *lyn* of *Othlyn* and the *mere* of *Dingesmere*).
- near a Viking Thing (the *ding* of *Dingesmere*).

So what about *Brun*?

In terms of our place-name evidence, this is surely our most essential must-have. Whether they connected it to a hill, a field, a ford, a fortification of some kind, or just left it by itself, a great many people remembered the place of the battle in conjunction with the word *Bruna* or *Brune*. This is why, as I said earlier, almost any place with the letters *B-R-N* in it has been suggested as the site of the legendary battle. Once more, though, linguists have shown us a way forward: scholarship has established, with near surety, that the words *Bruna* and *Brune* are, respectively, either a masculine personal name or a feminine river name in Old English. Furthermore, they've shown that the mysterious place-name *Brunanburh* isn't really missing from our maps at all: the Modern English town of Bromborough on the Wirral peninsula, which appears as *Brunburgh* in John Speed's 1611 map of the area, derives from Old English *Brunanburh*.[16]

BRUNANBURH ON THE WIRRAL

This discovery doesn't tell us that Bromborough was *the* Brunanburh, of course. It only tells us that Bromborough was *a* Brunanburh. For it to be *the* Brunanburh, we would need much more. To that end, there is copious socio-linguistic evidence that at the time of the battle the Wirral peninsula was split between a Viking enclave in the north and English influence in the south: a fitting place for a clash between them, just as *Ingimund's Saga* has it. Further narrowing the focus, the known folklore and archaeology of the Wirral, which includes previous attempts to locate the battle on the Wirral, indicates that the battle could have taken place somewhere on Bebington Heath, near Bromborough.[17]

More than that, the mid-Wirral fits our checklist here astonishingly well. It's on the correct side of England. It's a location relatively distant from major population centres but still on established lines of transport. Chester is the closest town of any size, and it's more than a dozen miles away along a Roman road that runs through the centre of the peninsula. The flat plains across the middle of the peninsula – judging by the geography and the historical place-names upon it – were in the tenth century largely uncultivated fields and woods. There seems to have been a significant Viking harbourage around a pool at its northern end, close beside a Thing that's still remembered in the village of Thingwall. Multiple place-names indicate local fords, including the Marfords, immediately west of Bromborough, which derives from Old English *(ge)mære + ford* (boundary ford). There are also multiple low hills and ridges in this same area that could merit remembrance, and a number of them were associated with religious practice, as was the case at Overchurch in Upton.[18] There are also several locations that could have been the site of a local fortification.

Collectively, this was enough to establish a working theory that Brunanburh took place on the Wirral, a conclusion that I supported in my 2011 essay, 'The Roads to Brunanburh', in which I presented the broad historical context for the battle, and an explanation for how the battle could have taken place on the Wirral: 'Those individuals seeking the battle site today', I wrote, 'might do best to seek out the heath along Red Hill Road. While local legends that the road was named for the blood that ran upon it are probably in error, there is nevertheless a decent chance that the paths here indeed ran red in 937.'[19]

Everything I knew – and everything most of my extraordinary fellow contributors to the *Brunanburh Casebook* knew – said that's where it was. As such, when I made the map for the book I placed a crossed-swords icon marking the battle-site on the fields west of Bebington and Bromborough on the Wirral. No question mark. No alternative. Here, the map said, is where it happened.

X marks the spot.

A year after the book was out, I visited the peninsula and took a picture of myself standing on Rest Hill Road (a couple of hundred feet from Red Hill Road), with the Clatterbrook valley behind me, on the other side of which the Viking lines would have taken position on that fateful day when they attacked Athelstan (Figure 20 in the plate section). I remained certain. The evidence we'd gathered – all of it – pointed to that one place.

Not everyone agreed with these conclusions. In the decade since the 2011 publication of the *Brunanburh Casebook*, I've received a fairly steady stream of antagonism for placing that X on our map.

An adherent of one alternative location accused me of being part of a 'Wirral Conspiracy'. A fair number of enthusiasts for alternative sites insisted that a 'Yank' had no business writing about English history. One person thought me a fool for completely failing to see the truth that the battle was fought on Dutch shores. Some cursed and condemned me in impressively colourful terms. Lost battles, like legends of lost ships and civilizations, spawn an extraordinarily passionate dedication – for some it can border on obsession – among those who devote themselves to finding the truth. Nothing better stokes enthusiasm than a case of unknowns.

None of this dedication is bad. It can be enormously useful when harnessed and channelled. And by far the greatest share of anti-Wirralists have been good people with, in their minds, legitimate objections to locating Brunanburh on the Wirral. These objections have, in turn, allowed us to strengthen the Wirral case – beginning with the issue of how large the armies were, and how they would have reached the battle-site in the first place.

9

The Ships and the Saga

From the beginning, the battle of Brunanburh would be noted for its size. The dead were 'countless', the most famous poem tells us: there was 'never greater slaughter' on the island.[1] Aethelweard, the nobleman writing a chronicle of England's history 40 years later, calls it 'a massive battle' that was 'still called "the great war"' in his day. Wulfstan of Winchester, a monk writing around the turn of the millennium, says there was 'a great slaughter'.[2] Eadmer of Canterbury, writing after the Norman Conquest, calls the alliance that Anlaf led to England 'an immense army'.[3]

When the sources provide actual numbers, they are surprising, to say the least. The poem that William of Malmesbury preserves in his account says Athelstan had 100,000 men in the field, and that 'Anlaf, alone of what were recently so many thousands, / fled the deposit of death'.[4] Similarly enormous in its numbers is the *Annals of Clonmacnoise*, which claims that at least 34,000 men died.[5] Medieval writers often exaggerate numbers in conflict, and these numbers seem very exaggerated indeed.

We can start working towards a more feasible estimate, however, by looking at the basic logistics of transportation. Writing in the early 12th century but believed to be using tenth-century sources, Symeon of Durham twice informs us that 615 ships were involved in the invasion.[6] This is a large number, but nothing as ludicrously staggering as 100,000 men on the English side. In fact, looking back through the reports of earlier large Viking fleets in the *Annals of Ulster*, we see them made up of 120 ships (in 837), 140 ships (in 849), 160 ships (in 852), and 200 ships (in 871). The *Anglo-Saxon Chronicle* lists some fleets that are even larger. In 851, a fleet of 350 ships raided up the Thames. A few decades later, in 893, two fleets of Vikings landed in south-east England. The first, landing near Lympne, was between 200 and 250 ships in size, depending on which version of the *Anglo-Saxon Chronicle* we trust, though a different source, the *Annals of St Neots*, says it was 350 ships. A related fleet, 80 ships strong, sailed up the Thames. A further 100 ships were sent by the Vikings of Northumbria and East Anglia to aid the first wave. Put together, this was an invading force of some 380 Viking ships in 893. Similarly, and missed by many, it appears that Symeon of Durham includes the kings from Scotland and Strathclyde in his ship-counting for the Brunanburh campaign: this, too, was a combined fleet.

That the Scots in particular came to Brunanburh by ship will surprise many – a younger me included![7] – but even the famous *Battle of Brunanburh* poem itself appears to say exactly this. The English, it says, gave

> hard hand-play to any heroes
> who with Anlaf over the sea-surge
> in the belly of a ship sought land,
> fated to fight. Five lay still
> on that battlefield – young kings
> by swords put to sleep – and seven also
> of Anlaf's earls, countless of the army,
> of sailors and Scotsmen.[8]

There is no differentiation made here between the two armies. The enemies of the English – Scots and Vikings both – came with Anlaf over the sea. Their departure is likewise presented, as the poem treats the Scots and Vikings as a single unified force, as 'hated peoples' who are 'hewed ... harshly from behind' during their attempt to flee.[9] After the poem describes the departure of Anlaf, who saved his life by taking to sea, it turns immediately to Constantine: 'So there also' – *swa þær eac* – 'the old one came in flight'.[10] Rather than distinguishing between their two flights, the poem situates them in the same place. After condemning Constantine and then Anlaf once more, the poet refers to 'the remnant of their army',[11] once more treating them as a unified force, before referring to 'the Northmen' – that is, the Vikings – departing on Dingesmere. Nothing is said of an overland Scots retreat, and the conclusion must be that with Constantine they joined the Vikings in this departure, which helps to explain how they were able to escape the carnage at all. It's true that large-scale Scots naval actions are few and far between until much later, but this hardly means that they were incapable of arranging naval transport for their armies. Scotland is surrounded by sea, and even if it hadn't had a strong naval presence in previous years, Athelstan's naval show of force in 934 would surely have impressed upon Constantine the need to develop these same capabilities. So while Symeon's invading force of 615 ships at Brunanburh would be significantly larger than other fleets, it isn't unreasonably so given the fact that this was the combined force of three allied kingdoms come by sea.

It could be that the numbers from *all* of our sources are too generous, of course, but this would seem to push scepticism too far. It's fair to reckon that Symeon was himself a *little* generous in his accounting – larger numbers of enemies make for a larger victory over them – but I see no reason to suspect he's off by a great deal. To keep the maths easy, let's call it 500 ships in the combined fleet.

But how many men in a ship?

The Battle of Brunanburh poem twice refers to the Viking ships as *knarrs*, a transport vessel that was often used by traders needing to move goods over the sea.[12] We don't know if this was simply because the term fitted his poetry or because he thought they really were knarrs. For that matter, we don't know how the poet would have defined such a term. An 11th-century example of what *we* call a knarr was discovered purposefully sunk in Roskilde Fjord. The remains of Skuldelev 1, as it is now called, have been raised from the seabed and can now be seen in the wonderful Viking Ship

Museum in Roskilde. It's believed to be a large example of the type: over 50 feet long and 15 feet wide at centreboards, it could carry more than 20 tons over the waves. Needing a crew of only a half-dozen experienced hands, a knarr such as this would indeed make a lot of sense for the moving of an army: at maximum capacity it could have potentially held close to 100 men in calm waters. Yet how representative Skuldelev 1 was of the average ship is unclear. The methods used in ship construction in the Middle Ages mean that we cannot set a definitive standard of size for any single ship-type. Adding to the problem, the ships involved in an invasion of this kind must surely have been of a wide variety: it was hardly the traditional 'longship full of Vikings' that we should imagine here. Any estimate will be unstable as hell, but if the ships altogether *averaged* around 50 men each, a 500-ship fleet could transport a maximum of around 25,000 individuals.

Even if an invading army meant to subsist as much as possible on the spoils of enemy territory, it would still need to bring with it an enormous amount of supplies, along with no small number of non-fighting personnel. Once more, we can only estimate what this would mean in reality – adding speculation atop our speculation – but in the end I would guess a combined invading force of, at most, 10,000 men, and more likely somewhere along the lines of 8,000 at best. This is not far at all from the numbers calculated by others who have studied the materials, which range between 5,000 and 10,000 men in the allied force.[13] If the numbers in William of Malmesbury's poem and in the *Annals of Clonmacnoise* have any basis in reality – I suspect they don't, but still – they would therefore be off by at least an order of magnitude. Athelstan responding with 100,000 men is impossible, but 10,000 might be possible. And while there couldn't have been 34,000 invaders dead on the field, 3,400 would not be a surprise.

We don't know the breakdown of the various allied forces – what percentage of the alliance was made up of Scots compared to the percentage made up of Vikings, and so forth. The degree to which Owain of Strathclyde is generally lost in the accounts of the battle probably indicates that he brought relatively smaller numbers of men to the fight, though it could also indicate the biases of our sources in recording it: more often than not, what people write down speaks to the concerns (and thus the enemies) of the present more than those of the past.

Whatever their composition, the three armies were all held together by their hatred of Athelstan and the English crown he wore. Sometime after Anlaf got back from Lough Ree, the Viking fleet set sail. The Scots and the men of Strathclyde were also on the move. As we've seen, Symeon of Durham and the great poem indicate that they, too, were on ships.

The Wirral would have been an excellent place for all three fleets to have met. No one was likely to have a difficult navigation, much less face threat from English forces. No one needed to sail around the North Sea. Anlaf had a straight shot across the Irish Sea from Dublin. Constantine and Owain both had straight shots down along the coastline from the north. All of these routes were safe, known, and fast: if the timeline was tight – and we have already seen that it was – then moving the men by sea would speed things along considerably.

If we *do* place Brunanburh on the Wirral, then we must find a place for 500 ships to land and bring these thousands of men ashore, a place to which Anlaf and the remnants of his army would flee after the battle in order to take flight on the sea.

We must find Dingesmere.

THE POOL OF THE THING

Linguists, demystifying the word itself, have showed that *dingesmere* was very likely associated with a Viking Thing, such as the Thing beside the modern town of Thingwall (which means 'meeting place of the assembly') on the Wirral. It has been suggested more specifically that *dingesmere* thereby means a wetland on the nearby shoreline of the Dee somewhere between Heswall Point and Ness.[14]

That the word references a Thing I don't doubt. That it could refer to the Thing on the Wirral – in light of all the other evidence already pointing to the peninsula – I also gratefully accept. But I see two significant problems with locating Dingesmere on the Dee estuary itself. First, while it's *possible* for *mere* to mean a coastal wetland, it's certainly not the most common meaning of the word. From a linguistic point of view, we should expect instead that it means a pool or body of water: standing water, not a sometime-marshy coastline. Second, the Dee estuary is a profoundly ill-advised place to harbour an invasion fleet. The most obvious problem is surely the exposure that the shoreline has to weather. Rough seas can throw boats into one another – or, worse, rip them from an anchor along a shoreline and take them out to sea. Brunanburh likely happened in October, after all, and the potentially rough weather of the autumn might have been the least of the reasons that Anlaf and his allies would have been fools to anchor on the Dee.

Let's start with the logistics. The Skuldelev 1 knarr that I mentioned in estimating the size of the allied army is over 15 feet broad. With 500 ships, that's nearly 7,500 feet of beach frontage in wood alone, not to mention the required spacing between them that would probably more than double it.[15] That comes out to around three *miles* of stretched shoreline. Just in terms of unloading supplies, this would be a nightmare. Worse, there were paths running from Chester up the western coast of the Wirral towards the port at Meols, which had been in use since Roman times. In fact, though one hasn't been found, it seems likely that a Roman road ran along this same shoreline. Roman road or not, the Dee estuary was arguably the easiest location on the Wirral peninsula for any English forces at Chester to threaten – that city was, after all, *built* on the Dee – which makes it one of the *last* places an invading force would want to come ashore. The enormous length of a landing on the Dee would also have weighed down the allies with an enormous defensive burden at a time when they could little afford it. Maintaining a defensive perimeter on even a single mile of beached fleet so accessible to the enemy would mean hundreds of men removed from the fighting force to stand constant guard on the ships. Anlaf and his allied commanders would know, after all, that the first step in making a landing is to establish control of the immediate beachhead: not just for the conducting of supplies and men to shore, but also for the maintenance of an escape route if things went poorly.

Speaking of which, a beach landing requires staking the ships to shore at high tide, which leaves them largely stranded until the next high tide. This can be useful for unloading supplies, but it's the worst possible scenario if trouble – like, say, losing the battle of Brunanburh – is encountered. In fact, across the end of September and early October – our prime window for the battle – low tide fell in the evenings, at the very point when we're told Anlaf was launching in flight from Dingesmere with the English in hot pursuit. If we knew the fleet was beached on a coastline, then this might actually give us a way to date the battle to a high-tide night ... but more likely the tides give us yet one more reason to think a beach landing likely. *No man is a fool*, you'll remember.

A far better alternative for Dingesmere is Wallasey Pool.

Like the Isle of Thanet upon which Anlaf's ancestors in the Great Viking Army landed – and by legend Athelstan's ancestors before them, giving birth to England – Wallasey (its name means 'island of the foreigner') is an island no more. Today, it's the north-east corner of the Wirral peninsula. Houses, parks, and roads – including the M53 as it snakes around Bidston Hill at the top of the peninsula's high-ground spine – unite what were once separate shores. What remains of the water that once kept them apart is Wallasey Pool, which enters the sea between Seacombe and Birkenhead.

That mouth, today narrowed by the modern industry of the docks that line the water's shores, was once well over a mile wide along the River Mersey and perhaps 20 feet deep in its channel. The pool itself ran inland to the north and west. At high tide, its waters likely reached the northern coast and drank of the Irish Sea. At low tide, paths probably ran across the north-west end of the Pool, connecting Wallasey to the mainland in much the same way that Hilbre Island, on the other side of the peninsula, is low-tide accessible today despite being more than a mile offshore. The ancient churches of St Oswald's in Bidston ('stone-settlement') and St Hilary's in Wallasey would have faced each other across the marsh and the Pool here.[16]

The tributary arms of the Pool, stretching west around the feet of Bidston Hill, would have grown increasingly shallow, spreading out like fingers woven into a reed-carpeted saltwater marsh. In the tenth century, this swampy area probably extended as far as Moreton ('marsh-settlement'). There were no doubt paths webbing through the marsh between the island's tidal channel and the rising ground of the peninsula, or reaching out from point to point across it – a low-tide path, for instance, might have run from St Oswald's to Overchurch on the other wide of the Fender. Such paths were passable for those who knew them, treacherous for those who did not. The draining of the old wetlands has covered most of this over, but fragments of the lost landscape can still be seen in the little ponds and thin waterways that are scattered across the Bidston Moss today. And place-names such as the hamlet of Ford – which was near Upton Station – and the Old Bank – near the confluence of the Fender and Birket – likewise hint at the past. In his 1922 study of the 'Wirral Watersheds', Eric Rideout reports local rumours that 'skulls, etc.' were found at the Old Bank, but no confirmation of this has been found.[17]

The ground, thus laid out, is strikingly similar to that of the battle of Maldon in Essex, which would take place a few decades later in 991. There, the Viking fleet landed at Northey Island, which was separated from the mainland by a low-tide ford. As the Vikings waited for the tides to shift for an attack on the upstream town of Maldon, the local militia was called out and lined up against them on the shoreline. When the tide dropped, the Vikings couldn't break the English defence of the exposed causeway, and the English couldn't cross it, either. Eventually, the Viking leader requested that his forces be allowed to cross to the mainland in order that a fair fight be made. The English lord, Byrhtnoth, owing to his *ofermode* – much debated, the word could mean pride or reckless courage – consented. In the ensuing battle of Maldon, Byrhtnoth and his men were wiped out.

The Vikings wouldn't be so lucky at the battle of Brunanburh, but their strategic landing at Wallasey Pool would be quite similar to the landing for Maldon.

THE ROADS

One of my maxims for understanding conflict is to *follow the roads*. Numerous local paths will exist between and among settlements, but armies on the move tend to follow wider, well-travelled arteries of transport. As we've already seen, this very often means following the preserved Roman roads.

Scholars have generally accepted that there were two such roads across the Wirral peninsula, though to date no definitive evidence of them has been recovered (something that is unfortunately true of most of the known Roman road network across Britain). Both of these roads would have led to the Northgate of Chester, which was founded as Deva Victrix in the first century.

The first road is thought to have run along the western coast of the peninsula, roughly following the line of today's A540. It terminated at the port of Meols, which was very active in Roman times. A great deal of transport between Chester and Meols would have no doubt taken place along the Dee, but the road would have had a compelling role as an alternative means of land access. It is this road that would have directly threatened any attempt to land on the western shore of the Wirral.

The second road is believed to have run from Chester to Mollington and then on to Ledsham, where it may underlie today's Ledsham Lane. Continuing northwards, it probably followed the line of Heath Lane and Street Hey in Willaston, before it's picked up again by Hargrave Lane. The proposed road is here overtaken by fields, but the Roman preference for straight roads would run it along the west edge of Clatterbridge Hospital, then across the M53 to where it appears again under Keepers Lane in Storeton. The presence of nearby Storeton Quarry, which is known to have provided stone for Roman work in Chester, may have been one reason for the road's existence. Beyond this point the path of the road enters the Preston Golf Club and things get hazy. There is a path and road called Roman Road on the other side of the fairways and greens, but it's unclear how far back that name goes. Certainly the way that this road curves looks distinctly non-Roman. After that, the build-up of modern construction leaves us in despair of recovering much evidence of an exact route. A relatively straight line would run the road almost directly up to the summit of Bidston Hill, so the assumption is that at some point beyond Prenton the road shifted westwards, tracing along the gentler slope past Noctorum. A spur might have taken off from here, crossing the Fender at Ford (perhaps an alternate road towards Meols?). It's all covered over now, but a good bet would be that the main road skirted Bidston Moss as it came around the foot of Bidston Hill – the paths through the marsh to Wallasey Island would have met it here – and thereby reached the head of Wallasey Pool. If the road continued to run eastwards along the southern shore of the Pool, it would line up quite neatly with a bridge discovered in Birkenhead during dock construction in 1845. Buried under 14 feet of silt, this three-span oak bridge, believed to be Roman in construction, would indicate a significant ancient interest in the region: crossing over a stream that ran northwards into the Pool, it was reportedly over 23 feet wide and 100 feet long.[18] It was located where Bridge Street terminates at Park Street today.

It may be that most of the ships in 937 would have anchored on the Wallasey shore of the Pool. The land on that side was probably firmer overall, and it certainly would put one more obstacle – the Pool itself – in the way of any English attempt to attack their ships.[19] If this is so, one can well imagine their camp-smoke rising around the area of Poulton, whose name means 'Pool-settlement'. That said, I would favour much of the landing coming ashore on the mainland side, with the immediate goal of securing of the road from Birkenhead. That road in hand, the allies would command a conduit into the heart of the Wirral and the waiting English lands beyond. Even better, a secured staging ground on the Birkenhead bank would make a retreat, if needed, more readily available. A campaign base on Wallasey, by comparison, would require retreating men to negotiate the paths through the marsh to the island, something that was only really feasible at low tide. This would already be a risky gamble, but if further retreat to the sea was required, any ships run aground could only be floated at *high* tide, which might be several hours away. If nothing else, the *Brunanburh* poem – with its report of the defeated army running to Dingesmere and immediately taking flight to sea – seems to square more readily with allied boats anchored on the mainland shore of Wallasey Pool.

One way or another, a better place to bring in the invading fleet could hardly be found. The Pool was protected from the weather. It was easy to reach and navigate. In the bays and brooks along its shores there would have been more than enough places to anchor without exposing the fleet along a long stretch of open beach. It also had a perfect combination of being secure from the English while still threatening them. Wallasey Pool was about as far from Chester as the allies could get, but the road down the Wirral enabled ready access to it. At the same time, the pinching of that road as it came around Bidston Moss created natural choke points for defence against attack: while a beach landing along the Dee would have required many hundreds of men to guard the ships alone, a landing in the Pool would have required a minimal expenditure of manpower to secure the entirety of the beachhead. Holding the road would have taken more than the three men who were able to hold the causeway at Maldon, but it was far easier than miles of open coastline close beside Chester.

What's more, we know that this end of the peninsula was, as *Ingimund's Saga* says, already established with Viking settlements in 937. Historically speaking, in fact, it is evident that the Wirral peninsula was split into two socio-linguistic communities: Viking to the north and west, English to the south and east. Though we've already seen how borders tend to be vague in the Middle Ages, it is worth noting that in this case the boundary between the regions might have been significant. Place-names still preserve its memory, as does the very DNA of long-time families on the peninsula.[20] So making a Wirral landing on the Pool – *ach linn* – meant having a friendly local populace who were more likely to aid in the establishing of the beachhead than fight it.

This was, quite literally, a safe harbour.

CAN WE TRUST EGIL?

We have the basic lie of the land. What comes next will require an answer to a key question: Can we trust *Egil's Saga*?

Of all the questions arising about Brunanburh, this is the one that vexes me most. Some scholars have attempted to find or reconstruct the battle relying entirely on the information provided in *Egil's Saga*. Other scholars have seen it as providing no reliable information whatsoever. And then there are a few who think that the battle it describes happening at Vinheithr isn't even Brunanburh at all.

Let's deal with this last issue first.

Egil's Saga traces about 150 years of history, ending its story around the year 1000. It is believed to have been written by Snorri Sturluson, who died in 1241. The saga's story of the battle was thus written about three centuries after the event ... which already raises a question about its trustworthiness.

The relevant section of *Egil's Saga* begins with Chapter 50. Athelstan is described as a new king (he was crowned in 924) threatened by 'Britons, Scots, and Irish' who rebel against English authority. Athelstan accordingly raises an army and forces them all to stand down. Sometime later, news of his successes reaches the brothers Egil and Thorolf as they are sailing near Flanders. They cross over to England with 300 fellow Vikings and are welcomed into the king's service.

So far so good. Athelstan was crowned in 924, and this sequence seems to fit well with the events after the death of Sihtric that resulted in the 'submissions' of the kings of Scotland, Bamburgh, Strathclyde, and Deheubarth at Penrith on 12 July 927. It likewise fits the fact that news of English power was spreading to the Continent: it was in 926, after all, that the king was welcoming an embassy from the son of Baldwin II of Flanders, who was trying to arrange a marriage to Athelstan's family.

Chapter 51 introduces Anlaf, a half-Scot, half-Danish descendant of Ragnar Lodbrok who would be the enemy of Athelstan in what the saga calls the battle of Vin-heath. The identity of Anlaf Guthfrithson's mother is unknown, but if she was remotely of

Scottish descent then this would likewise seem a perfect fit for the man Athelstan fights in the battle of Brunanburh. Perfect, that is, aside from the fact that *Egil's Saga* calls him the king of Scotland – which Anlaf entirely was not.

Anlaf the Scot invades Northumbria in Chapter 52. He kills a key English leader named Godric, while a second English leader named Alfgar flees. This success leads two brothers named Adils and Hring – previously local kings now reduced by Athelstan to the status of earls – to switch sides from the English to the Scots. Athelstan puts Egil and Thorolf in charge of the immediate defence while he gathers an army. Egil writes a poem:

Anlaf put one earl to flight
through furious battle,
and another felled;
a hard man in fight is this ruler.
Confounded on the field,
Godric trod a dark path.
This foe of the English
has half of Alfgar's lands.[21]

The identities of none of these men are certain. Godric looks suspiciously like an echo of Guthfrith, Anlaf's father who failed to seize control of York in 927, but Guthfrith died of sickness in 934. So it could be someone else entirely. Similarly, Adils looks as if he could be Idwal Foel, Welsh king of Gwynedd, who was forced to pay tribute with other princes in 926 and take the title of sub-king beneath Athelstan. We know of no brother of his named Hring, but he *did* switch sides against the English ... in 942. In that year, he and his brother Elisedd died attacking the English, who were now ruled by Athelstan's brother, Edmund.

THE BATTLE OF VIN-HEATH

As *Egil's Saga* continues, it moves to the heart of its battle account. In return for Anlaf stopping his army from further devastating

English lands, Athelstan offers him a winner-take-all battle. In one week, the two kings will meet on a field marked out by hazel rods (an old Viking custom, it seems) at a place called Vin-heath by Vin-wood. Anlaf agrees, and he moves his army towards the proposed battlefield. It's not made clear if he marches there or sails there, though it's clear that Vin-heath isn't the same location in Northumbria where he had killed Godric.

After his army's transport, Anlaf arrives in a town that sits north of Vin-heath, where the district provides him with suitable provisions for his forces. His position secure, he sends scouts south to Vin-heath itself, which is described as open, generally level ground with a river on one side and woods on the other. On their arrival, the scouts find English tents already pitched at the far end of this heath, where the river and woods grow closest. The English try to make it seem that they have more men present by pitching empty tents. The ruse works, and Anlaf's men pitch their own battle camp on their own end of the heath, slightly uphill from the English position:

> But where the distance was least between the forest and the river, and that was a very long way, there King Athelstan's men had pitched camp; their tents stood in all the space between the forest and the river... King Anlaf's men pitched their tents north of the hazel rods and there the ground had a slight downward slope.[22]

Despite the assurances of the saga-writer that such a practice was commonplace for armies, the idea of an arranged fight at an established location may seem strange to the modern reader. There is evidence, though, that this was indeed part of the practice of medieval warfare, perhaps because it ensured that combat would occur at a mutually identifiable, controlled location on the landscape. According to several versions of the *Anglo-Saxon Chronicle*, for instance, a raiding army of Danes encamped itself for several weeks in 1006 at Cwichelm's Barrow (today Scutchamer Knob, Easter Hundred, Oxfordshire). This had been a traditional assembly point for English armies, so it was thus a fitting place for the Vikings to challenge them to engage in a pitched battle. When the English failed to appear, the 'proud and not timid' Vikings marched over their countryside.[23] Nevertheless, our known instances of physically 'hazel-rodding' a conflict-site are for duels (called *holmganga*): this would certainly be in keeping with the arranged, winner-take-all nature of the fight.

After a week, Athelstan is still gathering forces and hasn't arrived for the battle. To buy time and delay an attack from Anlaf, the English offer terms to pay off the invaders. A truce of three days is declared in order to negotiate. When Anlaf finally declines the offer, the English produce even more generous terms. Another truce of three days is declared while this is debated between Anlaf and his commanders. Finally, a week after the initial battle date, Athelstan arrives in a town to the south that appears to be roughly an eight-hour ride from the field. With him are significant reinforcements. He rescinds all offers and declares the negotiations over.

In Chapter 53, Hring and Adils attempt a surprise attack against the English at dawn, but Thorolf's watchmen see them. He brings his men into position, as does Alfgar, who is back with the English despite his flight from the field earlier in Northumbria:

> Thorolf's forces were arrayed near the wood, while Alfgar's moved along the river. Earl Adils and his brother saw that they would not be able to come upon Thorolf unaware so they began to draw up their own forces. They formed up two groups as well and had two standards. Adils set his force against Earl Alfgar while Hring opposed the Vikings.[24]

Hring and Adils move ahead with their attack, and the bloodshed begins. As before, Alfgar flees. Adils, freed from facing the English force along the river, now wheels his men around and charges into Thorolf's flank. In response, the Viking bends his line so that his men, their backs to the wood, can defend against both Hring and Adils. In the ensuing melee, Thorolf impales Hring on a spear and holds the body up for all to see. His enemies break apart and retreat to their encampment. Adils in particular flees into the woods with some of his men.

Alfgar, meanwhile, fearing the retribution of Athelstan, bypasses the city south of the field and rides 'night and day' south and then west until he comes to a place called Earlsness. There he takes a ship to France, never to be seen in England again. This location is unknown, though a battle on the Wirral could mean that once we set aside the common poetic hyperbole of a day-and-night ride – the most that can be said is that it means the earl rode for a long time – this could be modern Ness, a port on the River Dee to the west and south.

Night falls. Athelstan has now arrived on the field. He sets up his own battle-camp, and for the next day's attack he assigns Egil to join him as 'the king's battalion formed up on the plain towards the river, while Thorolf's force moved to the higher ground along the wood'.[25] Egil is angry to be separated from his brother in this way.

Chapter 54 opens with the lines all advancing towards one another. Thorolf advances boldly, fighting well beyond the wall of his men. As the Viking pushes forward, Adils suddenly appears from the woods at his flank. Thorolf is killed.

An enraged Egil breaks from his side of the field and rushes across the heath. He attacks Adils, kills him, and presses the attack forward. Anlaf's position wavers, one entire side of his formation breaking up ahead of Egil's onslaught. Recognizing an enemy in disarray, Athelstan orders his men along the centre and river-side of the field to charge. The enemy panics into a rout. Anlaf is killed, 'and the greater part of the forces that he had'.[26]

The battle was over, but where had it been? When had it been? For that matter, *had* it been?

A Scots invasion of Northumbria would fit in 934, but Anlaf wouldn't have been there. He was certainly with the Scots when they invaded in the Brunanburh campaign in 937, and we might even excuse the saga confusing him for the king of Scotland, but neither Anlaf nor Constantine died that day. Idwal Foel, if he's behind the saga's Adils, was killed by the English in 942, but there were neither Scots nor a brother named Hring in that fight, and at that point both Anlaf and Athelstan were dead. On the other hand, if Idwal isn't behind Adils, we're left with even fewer connections to anything recognizably historical.

In the end, the historical roots of *Egil's Saga*'s battle of Vin-heath, if it has such roots at all, appear to run to several different episodes in time. At best, it looks like a kind of mash-up, rolling up some of England's greatest military hits in the period into one mega-hit that features the saga's two Viking heroes beneath the lights on centre-stage.

So those who see Vin-heath as wholly accurate to Brunanburh and those who see the saga's story as having nothing to do with it are equally wrong and right. It's part Brunanburh, but it's also part other things entirely. The real question for us, then, is *which* part is Brunanburh? It could be anything from just Anlaf's name to the details about the tactics of the battle and the topography on which they took place.

It turns out that both the tactics and the topography match well with a battle fought on the Wirral ... but it would be unwise to rely upon this information in making a case for this or any other location. *Egil's Saga* gives us a remarkable tale for the battle of Vin-heath, and in that fact alone is our biggest concern: Snorri's foremost purpose was not to inform history but to weave a story within history.[27] Egil himself was a real man, but that doesn't mean that every story about him is likewise real. And the warrior's poetry, as preserved in *Egil's Saga*, might also be real – preserved through the centuries on the lips of generations of northern storytellers – but that doesn't mean that Snorri wasn't filling in a lot of blanks when it came to where those poems were composed and what they were about.

Perhaps the Brunanburh campaign began with an initial attack from the Scots against Northumbria before they sailed for the Wirral. Perhaps an English leader named Godric was killed then. Perhaps such an attack was a distraction, intended to draw English eyes from the real target of the landings on the Wirral.

Or perhaps, despite everything said above, the target of the invasion really *was* York – just as so many want to assume it was – and the armies all planned to meet on the Roman road between the Ribble and that city. The northern armies from Strathclyde and Scotland might have marched down the western road from Carlisle, past Penrith, in order to meet the Vikings at Ribchester. Maybe there was an initial battle along this route. Maybe Athelstan really did offer up an alternative winner-takes-all, and the allied forces were transported to the Wirral – a literal ferry across the Mersey – and there Brunanburh happened.

This last possibility is the perfect storm for Brunanburh: it catches the most details from the most sources, and it paints a thrilling picture of what happened in 937. When I was asked to briefly imagine the battle for *Medieval Warfare Magazine* in 2020, I followed something very much like it. But in truth it's speculation atop assumption atop probability. We don't know if anything in *Egil's Saga* is really about our battle. It's perhaps. It's maybe. And it's maybe again.

But this doesn't mean we have nothing.

Our place-names clearly point us towards Brunanburh on the Wirral.

And the Wirral gives us roads. It gives us ground.

It gives us the means to understand the day England came of age.

The Day England Came of Age, 937

FOLLOW THE ROADS

Trying to get a higher view than his horse already provided, Anlaf lifted himself up from the saddle. The English banners were bolts of colour over the men marching up the road from Chester. Many of them carried spears, upright and tall, the metal flashing in the early morning sun. Commanders on horseback shouted orders, keeping the rabble militia in check, fanning them out as they reached the open heath, forming their line. It was too far to hear their words – and Anlaf wouldn't have understood much of their foreign tongue even if he could – but he could guess what they were saying. It would be the same things shouted by the commanders on his side. War was war.

Anlaf settled himself back into the saddle when he was sure of the biggest banner across the field. When he knew that the king himself had come.

From the moment he had leapt over the side of his ship and his boots had sunk into the soggy shore of Wallasey Pool, Anlaf's gaze had been fixed on the south. His army had found shelter and safety in the calm waters off the sea. The locals had welcomed distant cousins and friends. Their landing had been completely unopposed.

But it hadn't been a secret.

Athelstan had known an invasion was coming. Between traders and fishermen – to say nothing of outright spies – word of the preparations in Dublin would have spread across the Irish Sea. And the same word would have come down from the northern harbours where Constantine and Owain, and even the lesser lords on Man and the other isles, had been making their own preparations. Athelstan had known of the alliance, known it was setting sail. The blow was coming. He just didn't know where it would land.

And then hundreds of ships had sailed into Wallasey Pool. Hundreds of sails, white against the sky. Hundreds of wave-breaking prows. Thousands of armed men. There was no way to hide such a fleet, such an army, such an alliance. From the moment they'd come over the horizon, the English watchfires had been lit.

Anlaf had assured his fellow kings – long his enemies but for now his allies – that Athelstan would come in person. The king was too proud to let the challenge go unmet. He'd come, and they'd meet him together. They'd shove him back. They'd reclaim what he'd stolen from them. And if it meant giving Athelstan six feet of earth, so be it. They'd kill the king and cut a path into the heart of his fallen kingdom.

And now here the man was, a lamb to Anlaf's gathered wolves.

The only way it could have been more perfect would have been if they had been given an open road clear to Chester before the English army arrived. It would have been nice to storm that city, then watch from its walls as Athelstan helplessly flung himself at its gates – just as Aethelflaed had made Ingimund and the Vikings do a generation before.

Instead, the battle would be here, on the grassy heath that stretched down from the hill below his growing shield-wall.

His scouts had done well. It was a good place for a fight.

He had the high ground. His left flank was anchored against a reedy creek. His right flank was anchored against the line of woods. And he had enough men to fill the space with his wall, dense and strong.

It was fitting, too, that the charred husk of the English burh was so close beside the field.

Some English fortifications that Anlaf had seen were extensive, but out here on the frontier it was enough to build a shelter where threatened locals could find refuge with their lord ... or where a lord could find refuge from his threatening locals. This one had been little more than a farmhouse and outbuildings, but there had been a ditch, a wooden palisade and a blunted watchtower. There had been a signal fire that had been among those that warned of the coming of the alliance. The place was named, one of the locals had told him, for the little brown-stone brook beside it.

His men had burned it to the ground, of course. Even now, with the fires long out, the faint smell of ash drifted on the chill air, welcoming the enemy.

Anlaf smiled. It wasn't going to be the last fire he would set in England.

* * *

Following the presumed route of the Roman road from Wallasey Pool, there are a number of obvious places where the English would have preferred to stop the allied advance. On the shoreline would have been best, but the speed of the allied landing and the local support from the existing Viking enclave there would have made that difficult if not impossible. Barring that, choke points were possible anywhere along the road as it bent around Bidston Hill and turned south, towards Chester.

The further along the road we go, the more likely it is that the momentum of the invaders would have been counter-balanced by the gathering English response, which would have first come from Chester and then from greater Mercia as the alarm spread. There were almost assuredly some initial skirmishes as lines of local resistance tried to form up and were overrun – each one slowing the advance and giving time for the next line to grow stronger.

Our most essential source, the *Battle of Brunanburh* poem, indicates a final battleground some miles from Anlaf's ships. This certainly squares with our expectation that further along the road is better. As comprehensive as Alfred the Great's system of defence was, the English still needed time to put together an effective coordinated response. If one of William of Malmesbury's sources is trustworthy, in fact, Athelstan was initially stunned by the arrival of the alliance. While the king was frozen in shock:

> they defiled everything in their relentless plundering,
> afflicting the wretched fields with spreading fires.
> Verdant grass had withered on all the plains;
> diseased grain had mocked the prayers of farmers;
> so great was the barbaric force of the footmen and steeds.[1]

There's some exaggeration here, no doubt. This is the same poetic source that claimed how Athelstan, once roused, summoned 100,000 men to 'follow the standards leading to the stadium of war'.[2] This propagandistic quality should have us wary of the poem's pronouncements about the total destruction caused by the invaders, but it actually might make its reference to the king's hesitation more believable: for all that the poet was trying to trumpet Athelstan's glory, his initial lack of response might have been too well known to be denied.

Whether he was shocked or not, the English king was soon enough on the move. The Roman roads would have funnelled his men to Chester, then up into the Wirral peninsula to stabilize a growing front. That line, where the battle would happen, was drawn across the road at Brunanburh.

We have not yet found the burh. In the days before Alfred, a burh was little more than a defensible site, but as the period went on it became more indicative of a protective enclosure, likely around a small settlement or home.[3] Even as late as the 11th century, the protected enclosure – the burh – could be fortified by anything from a simple wooden palisade to elaborate masonry. A burh in the Wirral frontier is likely to have been small, leaving precious little in the way of lasting marks on the landscape. Worse, the same thing that makes terrain defensible often gives it great views, which means burhs were usually situated on prime real estate that continued to draw the eyes of the wealthy and powerful over time.

In such cases, the local burh could be buried beneath the local great hall.

Our best guess is that the remains of the actual Brunanburh are hidden beneath one of three later halls across the mid-Wirral: Poulton Hall, Storeton Hall, and Brimstage Hall. The first of these is nearest modern Bromborough, the second is almost atop the Roman road itself, and the third is in Brimstage, a place named in line with Bruna or Brune, combined with Old English *stæp* to mean 'Bruna's river-bank' or 'bank of the River Brune'.[4] Long-standing traditions of the Lancelyn Green family, owners of Poulton Hall since 1093, claim that the medieval ruins of a burh remain on part of their property. On the other hand, Storeton stands on the last stretch of high ground before the road drops down onto the open plain that extends to distant Chester. One of these or – less likely but still possible – none of them was the *burh* or *weorc* by which some would remember the battle.

Anlaf and his allies had the early advantage. As the English resistance solidified with Athelstan's arrival, it was the Vikings and the Scots who would choose the ground.

A BATTLE IS ITS GROUND

Athelstan, king of the English, gazed across the open plain. It was nowhere in particular, this place. No shadows of great cathedrals stretched over the tangled grass. No great wealth was here to be claimed. It wasn't in sight of any city walls.

It was merely where fate had brought him to his enemies.

Where *God* had brought him, he corrected himself. Years earlier, Hugh of the Franks had given him a crystal, etched with an image of the crucified Christ, enclosing a splinter of the very wood that had once held the weight of the Lord. The crystal hung from a golden chain about Athelstan's neck now. His fingers traced its edges. His lips whispered a silent prayer.

Of all the threats, this alliance was both the greatest and the least suspected. These men, who not long before had laid down their arms before him, had now taken them up again. Not just one of them in rebellion, but *all* of them in allied cause. He'd heard of the Welsh prophecy that this day would come, that the enemies of the English would set aside their enmities and come against him as one. He'd hardly believed it could be possible.

But here they were. There'd been skirmishes over the last few days as enemy scouting parties tested his strength and the firmness of his command, but this was the allied army in full. Thousands of men.

He could march no further. Neither could they.

It would be decided here.

His enemies had the high ground. Not much of it, but Athelstan knew better than to discount it. He'd directed that his own lines be drawn up where the road up from Chester forded a little brook that cut the field from west to east. It wasn't much of an obstacle – a man could jump across it – but it would be enough to prevent a charge if Anlaf got his men in order first.

After that, it would be a matter of who would break first. Either Athelstan would need to cross the brook and climb the slope to strike at his enemies ... or he'd have to draw them down and across those same obstacles.

The second option was best. His enemies were strong, but this was *his* ground. And that meant that every day he held his ground more Englishmen would come streaming up the roads from the south. His numbers would grow. He had no reason to rush.

But because this was his ground, every heartbeat he let the invaders stand upon it was an affront.

His fingers wrapped around the crystal, gripped it.

He would triumph, he reminded himself. God was on his side.

* * *

The battlefield is not hard to envision today. A thousand years has blurred the tenth-century landscape, but it hasn't erased it.

Place-names tell us that this stretch of ground was the boundary between the English and Norse socio-linguistic groups who split the Wirral almost in half. Behind Anlaf to the north and west was Viking land, the lot of Ingimund and his heirs. Behind Athelstan to south and east was Mercia, where Athelstan had grown up, which his father Edmund had died defending after putting down the revolt in Chester only 13 years before.

We can't rely on it, but it's striking how well this spot fits with the topography described in *Egil's Saga*. That tale reports how Anlaf's men were surprised to find Athelstan's camp when they approached the battleground, which suggests that terrain interfered with their sight-lines up to that point. Coming over a rise is likewise indicated by the saga-writer's suggestion that they made their camp where the land had a downward slope towards the enemy. This would place Anlaf's forward encampment in the vicinity of Storeton, which sits upon the divide between the watersheds of Wallasey and Bromborough Pools, where the land begins to slope southwards towards the place where the English would have made their stand. A field in this area is still locally called Bowman's Field, reportedly on account of the number of arrowheads found there. Whether such stories relate to Brunanburh – and whether if so they indicate the presence of the main battle-site or the location of what was undoubtedly a number of staged retreat points northwards up the Roman road – cannot be known for sure.

With the benefit of modern satellites and computer technology, we can look at this same stretch of ground in ways that Anlaf and Athelstan could only have sensed. We now know that a laser light, beamed at a target, will reflect upon contact with it. Because light travels at a constant speed, the time taken between the firing of the laser and its returning light can be readily calculated into a measurement of the distance between the laser and the target. Modern Lidar (a portmanteau of 'light' and 'radar') systems turn this simple principle into a massively powerful tool, providing a dataset of points that constitute the changing distance from that laser. Viewed in 3-D, this point cloud reveals the changing height of the ground. These dots can then be assembled into remarkably accurate depictions of real-world topography. Even better, we can use this same technology to erase vegetation and even modern buildings from the landscape to completely expose the raw terrain. When we're incredibly fortunate, this allows us to discover hidden features under the landscape that were made in the past: Lidar can be a great way for archaeologists to know where to dig.

We don't yet have the highest resolution Lidar point cloud for the Wirral. But even the 1m resolution scan presently available brings us closer to the battle than ever before. In Figure 21 in the plate section we see the result of combining these raw data points with colour to mark their respective heights from sea level. This is the end of the Wirral laid bare, with the wide line of the M53 (stripped of cars and signs) snaking around Bidston Hill like a vast ribbon. On top of this I've placed several overlays onto this raw image, marking out key features. We don't know the exact line of the Roman road – higher resolution Lidar, when it's available, might suss it out – but this rough approximation matches what we can see on the ground. This same methodology lies behind Map 5 (p. 166), which shows how the Roman road follows the high-ground of the ridge atop which Storeton Hall is built. From there it appears to run a line across the heath that's designed to intersect the two small streams in its path: Brimstage Brook and then a second brook, just near the bottom of the map, that runs out from Thornton Hough. In both cases, the probable line of road intersects these waterways where the geography points to a convenient crossing.

Without knowing the weather, we can't know how high these little streams were running at the time of the battle. We also don't know how wet the ground normally was around them, though we can at least make some guesses. Modern drainage techniques send water into designated channels. Confining water in this way makes it run faster – think about putting your thumb over the end of a running hose-pipe to make it spray – which in turn scours those channels deeper, carving steeper embankments. Absent this, we can imagine that in 937 – again, with the massive caveat of the weather – the land around these brooks was probably wetter, but that the streams themselves were shallower. There probably wasn't more moisture on the ground than there is today. Rather, the same level of moisture was more spread out.

Without uncovering physical evidence, we can't be sure whether the water crossings were fords or bridges. Romans used both.[5] We heard above about their extraordinary bridge-building abilities when the situation called for it, but bridges cost money to build, plus more money to maintain. This, added to the trickling nature of the little brooks on the Wirral heath, makes me suspect that the water crossings near the battle-site were more likely to be seen as a minor inconvenience than as an engineering challenge – so I've marked the road-crossings as probable fords. The northernmost of these, sitting upon the Brimstage ('riverbank of the Brune'), would seem a match for the *Bruneford* ('ford of the Brune') that is one of the two names given to the battle by William of Malmesbury. His other name for the fight, *Brunefeld* ('field of the Brune') would be the open heath through which these little watercourses make their unhurried way.

Aside from William's naming of the field, none of our sources mention a water crossing on or near the battlefield. This shouldn't surprise us much. Unless it had affected the battle's outcome, a little brook was just something that got your feet wet. And between the blood and the piss, feet always came out of battle wet.

Where would the lines have been drawn?

Though it clatters less than it apparently once did, the Clatterbrook still heads up the valley east of Storeton Hall today much as it presumably did in 937. As with Brimstage Brook – and another small tributary of the Clatter that rises from the ground nearby and curls around the front of Storeton Ridge near the motorway – this stream would not have been an insurmountable obstacle if the fight were imagined crossing it from bank to bank. Running a battle up and down its length, on the other hand, would be difficult. It seems reasonable to consider the Clatterbrook and its attendant reedy banks to mark the eastern edge of the battlefield.

The western side of the battlefield is less certain. Here, the rising ground was likely to mean a rising number of trees. At some point, any open field would have given way to clumps of woods like those that still dot the landscape between today's cleared fields. Truly flat and open ground isn't generally natural, so few battlefields are truly empty in the way that movie-makers tend to portray them. Copses of vegetation were neither obstacles to battle nor worthy of

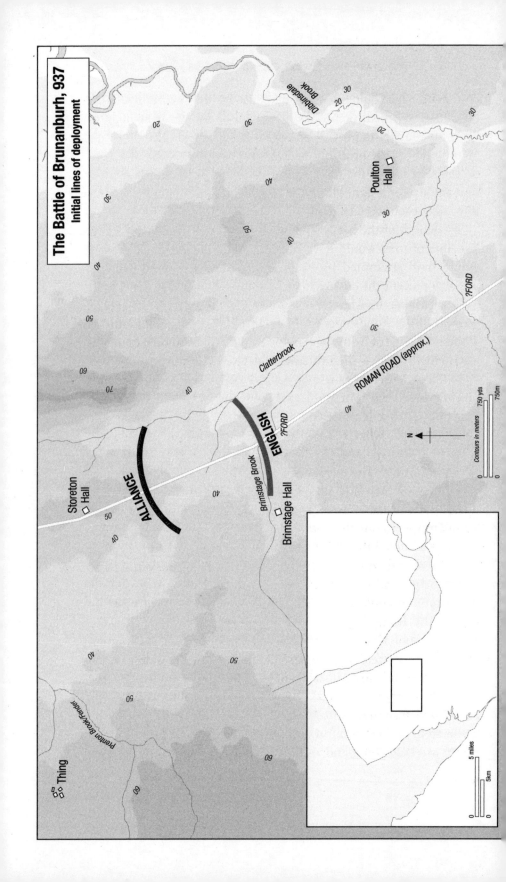

The Battle of Brunanburh, 937
Initial lines of deployment

Dibbinsdale Brook

20
30
30

30

20

30

Poulton
Hall

30

40

50

40

40

50

30

Clatterbrook

Roman Road (approx.)

?FORD

?FORD

ENGLISH

70

60

40

Brimstage Brook

50

40

Storeton
Hall

ALLIANCE

Brimstage Hall

40

N

Contours in meters

0   750 yds
0   750m

40

50

60

Prenton Brook/Fender

Thing

50

60

60

0   5 miles
0   5km

comment. Men could kill in the trees just as surely as they could kill on the grass. Like little brooks, trees could grow dense enough, or lined up enough, to provide an edge to a battlefield. The landscape of the mid-Wirral probably had just this in 937: a line of woods on the west side of the road, running roughly parallel to it. Armies drawing up for a fight along the road would have surely used this to protect their western flank.

The length of the battle-lines at Brunanburh depends on where that line of trees would have run: the commanders on both sides would have attempted to establish a river-to-woods frontage in order to prevent the enemy from outflanking their line. How great a distance it was between the Clatterbrook and the trees can only be guessed. If the woods opened up as far back from the Clatterbrook as today's village of Brimstage – which would make sense if there was a settlement there – then there would be a field maybe 3,000 feet wide. How densely men can be packed along such a front depends on their gear, their formation, and the tactics with which they will be deployed, but local period re-enactors from the Wirhalh Skip Felagr confirm what research elsewhere has shown: the average man in a shield-wall would take up at least three feet of lateral space along the front.[6] This would leave us with front-lines of perhaps 1,000 men on each side. Imagining the woods further away would open up the available space, as would changing the formation from a straight line to one that curves across the available landscape.

I have assumed that the allied forces reached the field first. They had a head start on the English, so they had the opportunity to select the ground that would be most to their advantage. Hardly better ground could be found than that just in front of Storeton Ridge. The Thing was just under one and a half miles to the west. Wallasey Pool was some six miles behind, though the marshy ground of its stretching fingers, depending on the tides, would have reached far closer in the valley of the Fender (called Prenton Brook in its upper stretches). The allied scouts would have quickly recognized that they could hold a line here that was unlikely to be flanked, on high ground with more high ground behind – this meant excellent command visibility as well as an aid to any strategic withdrawal. Athelstan, marching north up the road from Chester, had no choice but to react to the allied position.

Placing this position on what we've learned from our Lidar imagery, we can see how a curving line would be especially advantageous to Anlaf and his allies: they could fill the head of the valley from edge to edge with perhaps as many as 1,300 men abreast. This is the line on Map 5, roughly 4,000 feet long around its curve, in the optimal position upon the proposed field. Rank depth is a notoriously problematic area of research – so much depends on the tactics planned and the necessities of the terrain, to say nothing of troop training and morale – but a battle-line eight men deep would net a roughly 10,000-man allied army, close to what was estimated from Symeon of Durham's fleet of 615 ships between the invaders.

The English would have faced them, at some distance before the lines closed, in likely similar numbers. Only so many men would fit on the field. It didn't matter if they were English, Irish, Scottish or anything else. Measured against the ground, a man is simply a man.

It's unlikely we'll ever know where Athelstan initially drew up his troops. I suspect it was on the southern side of the ford across Brimstage Brook, perhaps along the path to whatever buildings there were – if any existed and hadn't already been burned to the ground – around where Brimstage Hall is now. Just over half a mile would have separated the two armies.

It's worth noting how the resulting topography seems to closely match what *Egil's Saga* tells us about its battle of Vin-heath. Anlaf was on slightly higher ground, facing the open space between river and woods. Athelstan filled the far end of that space, where it was slightly narrower. Whether the land between had been formally staked out with hazel rods, as *Egil's Saga* presents it, can't be known. But in truth it didn't matter. The field was set.

The fight would be here.

NO MAN IS A FOOL

The commander of an army is often likened to a chess-player. It makes sense: in battle, as in chess, the long game matters far more than the fate of a single pawn. We could also liken command to being in a fist-fight: a lot depends on deciding when to throw that first punch. Throw it too early, before you have your balance, and you might open yourself to a haymaker punch that knocks you out cold. Wait to throw it and it might literally be too late: while you were contemplating, the opponent's jab took you square in the jaw.

At Brunanburh, someone had to make the first move. Anlaf and his allies had the better ground. He and everyone else on the field knew they shouldn't abandon it. No one should help the enemy by playing into their hands. No one should wage war on disadvantageous terms.

But no battleground is level. No odds are truly even. Athelstan had the home field advantage. The army facing him couldn't do more damage than it had already done. It was bottled up. And every day that passed his own forces would likely grow stronger. He could afford to be patient. He shouldn't have made the first move, either, though he may have been emboldened by a belief that he had God's backing or greater numbers – or perhaps he was simply impatient to see it done. On the other side, we can also imagine Anlaf and the allies deciding to press the advantage of driving downhill into the enemy, of building momentum for an initial clash before the shield-walls settled in for the slog of the main fight.

In truth, what plans were laid that day, much less how they might have been communicated or carried out across the field of Brunanburh, we cannot know. To some degree, it doesn't matter. To approach battle with an eye only to the grand tactics of command is to stand apart from the reality of war as it was experienced by most of the men that day: shrunk down by the clouding miasma of battle, narrowed to the bare limits of the human senses – the line of one's sight, the reach of one's arm, the beating of one's heart. To be in that fog, for those who have known its chemical rush, is to be at once hypnotized and horrified by the reduction of the world's complexity to the simple immediacy of the moment between life and death. It wasn't about the grand schemes of command. It was the weight of the weapon, the lightness of the linden-wood shield, the pressure of the men beside and behind, the anger of the men ahead.

Whatever speeches might have been given, whatever prayers might have been said, the final truth was that each man was led first by his fear. Of death. Of shame. For some, that fear might have spurred bold action, but even among the most experienced fighters this cannot have been common. From the hours before the battle, through the day of bloodshed, to the fall of night that replaced the clash of steel with the moans of the dying, there was but one thing on the minds of most of the men: the desperate need to survive. What kept a man from fleeing the terrible field, from running to the safety of the immediate trees or down the road to distant homes wasn't patriotism or duty or any sense that their cause was just. No. What kept him facing the enemy, boots pushing forward, was his determination that the best chance for survival was to do just that. He felt, in the presence of the men to his left and to his right, safer than he would feel with his back to the enemy.

It began, most likely, with shouts. Perhaps the poets came forth, men like Egil, who staked their metaphorical flags over the field in the provocatory boasts of their *flytings*. Shouts would have been raised behind them, the cries meant to instil unity in friends, fear in foes. Atop the voices came the rattling, crashing, clanging noise of rattling spears, of axes and swords on shields. The lines were only a few hundred yards apart. Close enough for the voices to carry. Far enough for the arrows not to reach.

The command to move forward – whichever side gave it – must have been passed through the lines. Did animal horns signal the forward march? Was the word passed man to man between the allies, then officer to officer down the ranks? How could commands even be heard through the tumult? Could the Scots have understood the commands of the Vikings if they gave them? We don't know.

They approached each other. Foot by foot. The meeting of shield-walls is not the cinematic drama of sweeping cavalry or charging men. It is the slow collision of two great masses, the sliding glacier meeting the rising sea. Arrows were loosed once range was reached. Only a few at first, solitary whistles cutting the air. But as the first of them fell into the closing lines of men they summoned up hundreds more in their wake. The air hummed with death.

Closer still and men threw darts and slung rocks. More and more the arrows found their marks: slipping between raised shields or blasting through their splintered backs into the flesh of cowering men.

Men of wealth had armour to protect them: helmets and mail shirts buckled tight over layers of wool. Many more men had only their round shields to protect them: stout planks of linden-wood rimmed with iron. Some might have had little protection beyond their faith in gods or good luck.

The lines came together. It's horrifying to imagine what it was like for the men on the field. Those in the front line – bracing the shields as they crashed into one another, dodging the points of the swords and axes and spears shoved through the cracks – were close enough to smell the breath of the enemy. Whether the ground had been dry or wet, it turned to mud within minutes: piss and shit, blood and spit all mixed at their feet. When the wall shifted, the feet seeking traction left legs outstretched and in reach of the enemy. Steel glinted towards the exposed limbs. Spearpoints drove into thighs. Blades reached behind knees, slicing tendons. If a man went down, the gap he made was filled at once. Success depended on the wall holding.

For hours, if we believe the poem, they strained against each other, the men heaving against their shields, stepping on the bodies of fallen friends who sank ever deeper into the earth. Now and again the lines might have pulled apart from one another to close gaps in the walls and attempt volleys of arrows at each other, but always they came back with a roar ripped from parched throats. To the gathering ravens watching from above, it would have looked like two mighty jaws opening to reveal a red maw, the field taking a deep breath before the jaws slammed back together – thousands of metal teeth grinding up the soil and the bodies caught between them. That it went on so long points to how evenly matched the struggle was. It could have gone either way.

Eventually, as the shadows lengthened, the allied line wavered. We don't know why. It could have been exhaustion. It could have been that one of its leaders gambled on some kind of desperate assault and failed. Whatever it was, it opened a gap in the line that couldn't be filled. As the *Brunanburh* poem says, the English split the shield-wall of their enemies – *bordweal clufan*, in the Old English.

The end, after so much fighting, would have been mercifully quick.

As the victorious English surged into that flash of a gap, the battle played out in a fashion common to most medieval infantry battles: the breached line split, folded back, then broke altogether. Driven by panic, the rout began.

* * *

Of course, we could dream up far more complex scenarios. One alternative put forward begins with almost exactly this same position for the allied lines, but suggests that Athelstan goaded Anlaf down from the higher ground by making the left side of his line (that is, his western flank against the woods) appear weak and vulnerable. Anlaf, taking the bait, charged down in the hope that he could break that side of the English line and wheel into the English flank. For a moment, the theory goes, this would have seemed to work. Athelstan had to wheel his lines so that their backs were against the Clatterbrook to defend against the attacks now coming from north and west, and it was in this perilous position that the English king can be imagined signalling for a mounted force that he had hidden behind Brimstage. At the signal this cavalry rode out and smashed into the rear of the allied force, routing them and winning the day.[7] This scenario is close to what *Egil's Saga* says happened when Adils attempted to wheel around against Thorolf after Alfgar had (once again) fled the field: there the surprise attack into the enemy rear came not from a cavalry but from Thorolf's brother, Egil. But the truth is that we have no notion of the actual tactical decisions made at Brunanburh. We don't even know something as simple as 'Who attacked first?' The dramatic scenario might be true. My more prosaic explanation might be true. Or neither of them might be true. All we really know is this: The armies met at a place called Brunanburh. The loss of life was extraordinary. The allies turned and ran. As the *Battle of Brunanburh* poem says:

Here King Athelstan, lord of earls,
ring-giver of men, and his brother also,
Prince Edmund, age-long glory
won in strife with swords' edges
near Brunanburh. They split the shield-wall,
hewed the battle-wood with hammer-beaten blades,
Edward's sons, as it was their
birthright that they often in battle
against every enemy defended the land,
treasure, and homes. Their enemies perished.
The men of the Scots and the men of the sea,
fated, they fell. The field darkened
with the blood of men, from the rising of the sun
in the morningtime, when that glorious light
glided over the ground, bright candle of God,
of the eternal Lord, until that noble creation
sank to rest. There lay many warriors
destroyed by spears, men of the north
shot over shield, and so, too, the Scots,
weary, sated with war.[8]

Until hard evidence is found to provide a tighter location, topography and tactical considerations point to the fields south-west of Red Hill Road as the place where the left end of Anlaf's shield-wall formed up. The English forces were lined up opposite them to the south. In 937 this heath was wet with blood of friend and foe.

MEN MOVE LIKE WATER

The famed poem from the *Anglo-Saxon Chronicle* reports that when their lines were broken the allied leaders undertook a difficult flight to the sea after the battle:

> The West Saxons thence
> the length of the day in troops
> pursued the hated peoples,
> hewed the fugitive harshly from behind
> with mill-sharpened swords. The Mercians did not deny
> hard hand-play to any heroes
> who with Anlaf over the sea-surge
> in the belly of a ship had sought land,
> fated to fight. Five lay still
> on that battlefield – young kings
> by swords put to sleep – and seven also
> of Anlaf's earls, countless of the army,
> of sailors and Scotsmen. There was put to flight
> the Northmen's chief, driven by need
> to the ship's prow with a little band.
> He shoved the ship to sea. The king disappeared
> on the dark flood. His own life he saved.
> So there also the old one came in flight
> to his home in the north; Constantine,
> that hoary-haired warrior, had no cause to exult
> at the meeting of swords: he was shorn of his kin,
> deprived of his friends on the field,
> bereft in the fray, and his son behind
> on the place of slaughter, with wounds ground to pieces,
> too young in battle. He could make no boast,
> that gray-haired warrior of the sword-slaughter,
> the old deceitful one, no more than could Anlaf.
> The remnant of their army had no reason to laugh
> that they were better in the work of war
> on the battlefield, of the clashing of banners,

of the meeting of spears, of the meeting of men,
of the exchange of weapons, when they on the field of death
played with the sons of Edward.
Departed then the Northmen in their nailed ships,
dreary survivors of the spears, on Dingismere,
over deep water to seek Dublin,
back to Ireland, ashamed in spirit.[9]

Barring other evidence coming to light, we have to assume that
this flight was almost entirely taken north, following the existing
road. The road meant speed, but it also meant familiarity: this
was the route that Anlaf and his allies had used to reach the field.
Retreating by it, rather than over unknown ground, is expected.
For these same reasons, north would be most directly away from
the English forces. In the absence of other factors, combatants are
most likely to flee a fight by 180 degrees, not 90. Aside from this
following instinct, it also follows simple common sense: the only
route they knew was the route they had taken; flight in any other
direction meant plunging into unknown territory with uncertain
dangers. It hardly needs to be said, but a flight north along the
road would once again place *Dingismere* somewhere on the north-
eastern corner of the Wirral – the very same Wallasey Pool for
which I have already argued.

The field they fled was a charnel house. The *Annals of Ulster*
describes 'many thousands' of dead, and this could well have been
so. Some may have been left to rot or be torn apart by animals – the
Brunanburh poem says as much – while some may have found their
eternal rest in mass burial pits. Others would have been accorded
more honour – particularly dead English noblemen. While some
of these might have been transported to crypts elsewhere in the
region, it stands to reason that at least some of the dead were buried
in the nearest consecrated ground. Closest to the battlefield would
have been St Andrew's Church in Bebington, about one-and-
a-half miles east, which was the site of an Anglo-Saxon chapel.
Francis W. T. Tudsbery, who in his 1907 book *Brunanburh A.D.
937* appears to be the first to locate the battle of Brunanburh in

the general location provided here (though hardly matching in all respects), records the finding of undated bones on the grounds of Storeton Hall and Brimstage Hall – not unexpected stories of the Victorian era – as well as skeletons with arrowheads at St Andrew's Church 'some thirty-five years ago'.[10] Unfortunately, because none of these supposed physical remains have been identified, none have been dated and examined, leaving them for now no more reliable to the historians than whispers of ghosts.

It's likely that the allies, as they retreated towards Wallasey Pool, made several attempts to stage their retreat by forming up defensive lines at choke points where the sacrifice of a few could save the lives of many, including one narrowing along the road as it passed through where Prenton stands today.[11] Wherever the road actually routed through this area, gullies and slopes would have narrowed the passage considerably. Another choke point might be behind the reports mentioned in the last chapter that 'skulls, etc' were once found at the Old Bank where the river Fender, running north from the battlefield, met the Birket, running east into the Pool. Whatever they were, the efforts to stop the English pursuit would have been desperate acts undertaken in the bloodiest chaos.

> They left behind to divide the corpses
> the dark-coated one, the black raven,
> the horn-beaked one, and the dusk-coated one:
> the white-tailed eagle, to enjoy the carrion,
> that greedy war-hawk, and that grey beast,
> the wolf of the wood. Never was there greater slaughter
> on this island, never as many
> folk felled before this
> by the swords' edges, as those books tell us,
> old authorities, since here from the east
> the Angles and Saxons came ashore.
> Over the broad salt-sea they sought Britain,
> those proud war-smiths. They overcame the Welsh,
> glory-eager earls, and took hold of this land.[12]

* * *

It's a common refrain among many English scholars that Athelstan's win over his enemies was total and dominating: a 'crushing' victory.

A victory it was, yes.

But crushing it was not.

How hard a fight Brunanburh had been – how utterly close it had come to going the other way – is clear not just from the all-day nature of the battle, but also from what happened next. After his enemies fled the field, Athelstan didn't pursue vengeance. There was no campaign of retribution into Scotland or Strathclyde. No call for a new political submission was given. When they left Brunanburh, he left, too: back to safety, accompanying the bodies of the nobles who had died. Among them were two sons of his uncle Aethelweard (not to be confused with the chronicler), named Aelfwin and Aethelwin. William of Malmesbury, who presumably was in a position to know, says they were interred at Malmesbury Abbey.

As it was with the army's advance march towards the battle, our sources say nothing of places visited on its return march from Brunanburh. This stands quite against the situation of just three years earlier, in 934, where we were told of Athelstan's visitation to multiple sites to and from his fights against Constantine in the north. The impression we are given isn't that Brunanburh was on some distant hill far from the heart of Athelstan's kingdom. It was close. The *Brunanburh* poem says the English 'defended the land, treasure, and homes' that were 'their birthright'.[13] Henry of Huntingdon says they had to 'defend the hoards and homes of their native land'.[14] William of Malmesbury describes an alliance that 'had advanced far into England'.[15]

The only *certain* pieces of information we have about the field at Brunanburh – the place-names by which it was known in the immediate years afterwards – unquestionably point us to blood being shed in the mid-Wirral. It was near enough to Athelstan's centre of power not to merit remarks about the march. That proximity also fits the shared goal of the grand alliance that had come to the fight: not what Anlaf alone desired, but what could bring three nations so recently at war with one another to the very same side of the battlefield. It was an attack on the heart of England itself, an assault on the imperial pretentions of Athelstan.

* * *

In sum, this is my best guess of where it was and how it was.

Like an investigator of the car crash we talked about in the introduction to this book, I have made my conclusion based on the evidence before me. It is a report about what happened, but it cannot encompass the whole truth. And if more information presents itself, the investigation will need to be re-opened.

What new evidence could we expect? It's doubtful that a new tenth-century account will be found. Instead, our best hope for new information must be the earth itself. The evidence of linguistics, tactics, and other points of triangulation has carried us this far. We can't always find physical, testable remains, but if we did then they might, as we said above, give us the smoking gun (or shivered arrow, as the case may be).

Wirral Archaeology

So many of those who have written to me in anger don't understand the core drive of the historian. 'You're scared of what being wrong would do to your career!' they often say. Hardly so. As historians, we aim not to *be* right, but to *get* it right. This is especially the case in something as full of questions as Brunanburh has been, where identifying the site would enable me to begin work on questions that fascinate me far more than the *where*: how did the armies get there? How does the location fit our sources? Was *Egil's Saga* even remotely accurate? How can we reconstruct the battle?

Of course, being right *and* getting the chance to start addressing those next questions might be the best situation of all. And there is a chance that what Wirral Archaeology has been finding will be the key to just that.

Wirral Archaeology began as a loosely coordinated gathering of passionate enthusiasts, but over the years they've grown unquestionably more professional, more learned, more *serious*. They've done tremendous work trying to find the route of the Roman road through the Wirral. They've also worked to get the funding necessary to investigate a Viking ship that was reportedly unearthed and then reburied during the building of a pub in Meols in 1938. Since the late 1980s they have been interested in the theory that Brunanburh might have occurred somewhere on the Wirral: in addition to a handful of academic musings, local lore talked of an 'ancient battlefield' in the area. The 2011 publication of the *Brunanburh Casebook*, as they have said, 'acted as a supercharger' for their investigations of the battle.[1] The arguments outlined in the *Casebook* might have been convincing enough for them, but they realized that other folks were going to need proof – so Wirral Archaeology set their minds to finding just that.

In evenings after work, on weekends between other business, with apologies to loved ones for going out *again*, they put on their boots and headed out into the fields. Armed with metal detectors, maps, even a magnetometer they managed to purchase, field by field they got the permissions necessary to do some initial scans and put shovels into the ground when needed. They looked under the 'X' on the *Casebook*'s map.

As confident as I was in my early Brunanburh research, the chances of finding artefacts from *any* battle are astonishingly small. Battles don't leave large-scale remnants. Soil chemistry and time often destroy what few remains there are. So I would have said that the chances that they would actually find things were vanishingly small.

Soon enough, though, objects began coming to light. One area, called Field 3, offered up thousands of artefacts.

One of the first lessons of archaeology is that artefacts rarely come out of the ground looking like the cleaned-up pieces one sees at the British Museum. The centuries rot precious evidence away or encrust it with layers of corrosion. Initial finds thus present something of a Rorschach Test for the observer: what one sees in them is often a function of what one expects to see in them. If someone is looking for arrowheads, for instance, it's rather tempting to see an arrowhead in anything roughly shaped that way. This makes for a constant struggle as one balances the excitement of the search with the scientific detachment of not imprinting a definition on the somewhat abstract forms being uncovered.

Archaeologists have processes to turn raw finds into positive identifications. Some of it is old-fashioned comparative work between the current object and other known objects, but there are also an increasing number of technological advances in the field: scans and tests that can reveal not just an object's hidden structure, but also the elemental composition of that structure. We can confirm that an object is an arrowhead, for example, and we can even make some solid estimates about when and where it was made. The one thing all these processes have in common is a need for expertise and a great deal of time.

And, perhaps worst of all, *funding* – which is often the single biggest hurdle that a small organization like Wirral Archaeology faces.

When I first encountered their findings in July 2019, that lack of funding meant the artefacts hadn't been subject to study. They were simply rows upon rows of artefacts in their raw form: bagged and tagged with GPS coordinates and other information, but otherwise one inkblot test after another.

It was clear that not all of it was medieval – littering is hardly a modern invention, so archaeologists find a lot of other things on their way down – but some of it looked as if it probably was. Most of *that*, in turn, looked as if it was broken bits of refuse. This wasn't at all surprising: the fact that archaeologists study what people left behind means that, by and large, they study refuse even when they get to what they're looking for. In this case, many of the medieval-looking pieces – no dates were then known – appeared to be associated with metalwork: hammers and chisels, along with what looked like slag. But here and there were items that looked like bits of weaponry. Parts of blades, maybe. Things that looked like arrowheads.

Again, however, what an artefact *looks like* and what it *is* can be two very different things. Artefacts that look important might be junk. Some that appear to be junk might be incredibly important. In the year following my first visit, interest in Wirral Archaeology's findings – they had recovered some 4,000 objects at that point – was sufficient for Wirral Borough Council to commission an initial professional report on the project, co-authored by Paul Sherman, Clare Downham, and Robert Philpott. This capable team was able to make a preliminary analysis of a number of the most promising objects. The results were fascinating.

Figure 29 in the plate section shows Artefact WA2415, a Scandinavian arrowhead, made of iron, classified as Halpin type 1 (Jessop type T1/Wegraus type A). One edge of the blade is chipped, and its stem is slightly bent, suggesting that it may have been damaged in battle. Over 80 per cent of the arrowheads connected to Irish contexts before 950 match this type. It is, in other words, exactly the kind of arrowhead that we would expect Anlaf's Viking forces from Ireland to have utilized.[2]

How deceptive corrosion can be is evident in Figure 30, which shows Artefact WA42. At a glance this appears to be a socketed arrowhead (Jessop type MP3), but X-ray analysis revealed that the 'socket' is the result of corrosion built up along its tang. Despite their differences in outer appearance, then, this arrowhead is of similar design to WA2415.

As exciting as the arrowheads are, the artefact that most raised our eyebrows when we first saw the findings was WA21 (Figure 31). Subsequent analysis has shown that this is a decorative strap end (Thomas type B), made of copper, with zoomorphic shape. It dates to between the mid-eighth and 11th centuries: a perfect frame for Brunanburh, and a very tangible human connection to the past.

Also bringing us closer to the past are the gaming pieces found by Wirral Archaeology, like the assortment pictured in Figure 32. Military camps are not generally the subject of record in our written sources, but we do have a surviving description of the inevitable gambling in Guillaume Guiart's eyewitness description of an encampment in 1304:

The scoundrels, who carry their dice,
Will not cease to play their games.
Many commence great shouting
At each deception:
From the complaints, fights, and false marks
Scoundrels are chased away from such places,
All who get what's coming to them;
Whichever game of chance is played,

They desire to have an advantage.
This one places his bet on the game,
And the other counters with coins;
The one calls for seven, the other matches:
The one who wins grabs from the other,
And the loser cries and shouts.
One blasphemes and swears
On the blood, liver, and guts,
That, as everyone knows,
His silver was set on seven,
And his companions were on four.[3]

While they may appear to be formless, these artefacts would have been a common sight on a medieval army campaign, just as their modern equivalents of time-passing distraction are common to military encampments today.

The process of evaluating these and the many other artefacts is very much still in its infancy – we cannot and should not jump to conclusions – but it is already evident that some of the artefacts match the period and the profile of the Brunanburh campaign. They are only a fraction of the thousands of artefacts so far recovered, however. Many other objects that at first glance looked like blades or the heads of arrows or spears turned out to be nothing more than corroded pieces of iron – hardly weapons of war. In fact, the majority of what the team has thus far examined appears to be metalworking debris.

The thing is, a smith is unlikely to set up shop in the middle of nowhere. And while modern development has brought homes within view of Field 3, there's no known earlier settlement in the vicinity that would explain having such a concentration of remains. Nor are the finds located where one could expect that water or other forces had pushed them all together.

A working hypothesis at present is that Field 3 marks the site of a medieval military encampment. Moreover, it must have been an encampment associated with a force of significant size. Small raiding parties don't engage in metalworking at the scale necessary to leave a high number of artefacts strewn about. On top of this, some of the remains appear to be the result of active smelting: bloomeries and hearths can be field-built on campaigns, but doing so requires significant effort.

So *if* Wirral Archaeology has found an encampment, it's the encampment of a massive, pre-950 army that had a *lot* of metalwork to do involving Viking remains in the mid-Wirral. Not a lot of candidate events can fit that bill, but Brunanburh certainly does. Field 3, at least to the time of this writing, looks very much like what we'd expect for the kind of post-battle recycling described at the beginning of this book.

Field 3 would thereby locate the general vicinity of one of Athelstan's camps, roughly two-thirds of the way along a straight line between the hillside where I have suggested Anlaf and his allies established their lines and Poulton Hall, which is itself situated on a low hill that overlooks the Marfords and the modern town of Bromborough to the east. As it happens, the flat promontory that Poulton Hall commands, bounded by the ravine of Dibbindale Brook, is one of our prime suspects for the location of the Anglo-Saxon *burh* that would have given the area its name; the traditions within the Lancelyn Green family that the ruins of a medieval fortification (*burh*) remain on their property would support this.[4] If confirmed by modern archaeological surveys, it may be that Brunanburh itself – not just the battle, but its namesake – may also be coming into view.

THE CONTINUING SEARCH

As we learned when looking at the reconstruction toolkit of the conflict analyst, archaeology has much to offer, but it takes time. The finds uncovered are still in the process of being studied, and Wirral Archaeology continues to search for more as they are able.

Encouragingly, more landowners are opening their fields to the search, which should enable archaeologists to bring the hunt ever closer to what we believe to be the actual site of the battle. At time of writing, an artefact that had already been found near

Clatterbridge and initially thought to be a late Roman spearhead has been archaeologically identified as a mandrel, a tool that was used to form the sockets on spearheads, just like the ones that were taken to battle in 937. In the coming years, we may view this as the literal tip of the spear when it came to finding proven battle-remains of Brunanburh.

Material evidence isn't necessary to conclude that the battle of Brunanburh happened on the Wirral, but it's nevertheless remarkable that these continuing discoveries fit with the story that we already have from the sources, the history, and even the topography of the ground itself: here, in 937, Athelstan won his victory.

But to what end? What makes this battle, of all the ones that the king fought, so important?

England, Come of Age

The stakes at Brunanburh were no less than the survival of England. The grand alliance of nations around the Irish Sea had come together to destroy Athelstan. Constantine and Owain weren't taking their armies into battle to do Anlaf a favour. This was for them, as it was for anyone in battle, a life and death struggle.

Constantine left his son dead in the field. He would never again threaten the English. In 943 he abdicated the throne – probably unwillingly – and became a priest. He died in 952. Scotland's relationship with England would remain tense for centuries: the border between them as it stands today was more or less established by the Treaty of York in 1237, but even that didn't end conflict between the realms.

Owain, the king of Strathclyde, disappears from the record after Brunanburh. It's possible he died on the battlefield. His successors would continue to struggle to keep the kingdom alive, but it was ultimately in vain. Strathclyde was subsumed into Scotland in the 12th century.

Anlaf reappeared in Ireland a year after his defeat at Brunanburh. Perhaps he spent the winter with Constantine in Scotland, licking his wounds. Perhaps he went elsewhere. Perhaps he was in and out of Dublin and the records aren't complete enough to cover his whereabouts. We just don't know. Sometimes the sources we rely on are like a security camera fixed on the street: it might pick up someone passing by, but it doesn't tell us what they were doing before or after they were in frame.

Athelstan was at the height of his glory. He could now boast, as many of his coins had already declared, that he was *rex totius Britanniae* (king of all Britain). No longer just a dream, this was an England come of age: grown into something like what we imagine today. Historian David Dumville has summed up the king's importance with the simple statement that at Brunanburh 'Athelstan became the father of mediaeval and modern England'.[1]

The anonymous poet behind the poem *Rex pius Athelstan* (Devout King Athelstan), probably writing in the immediate aftermath of Brunanburh, seizes the moment to compare the victorious king to Joshua, the martial king of the Old Testament who finally conquered the Promised Land for God's chosen people:

> O devout King Athelstan, famed across the widespread orb,
> whose glory thrives and whose renown endures everywhere,
> whom God made king of the English, resting on the foundation
> of the throne, and ruler over earthly beings,
> clearly so that this king himself, strong in war,
> might conquer defiant kings, treading upon their arrogant
> necks.[2]

The poet here references the story of Israel's final defeat of the five kings of the Amorites, where Joshua has the defeated leaders of Canaan brought forth and instructs his men to 'go and set your feet on the necks of these kings' before he executes them.[3] The association of Athelstan with Joshua is an obviously flattering one for both king and country, as it also associates the English with God's chosen people, the Israelites. The biblical reference is perhaps doubly fitting given the five young kings Athelstan had slain on the field according to the *Brunanburh* poem.[4] Similar sentiments comparing these two warriors of faith, Athelstan and the Israelite leader who would in time become one of the famed 'Nine Worthies' of the Middle Ages, quickly propagated.[5] Athelstan, whose royal styles after Brunanburh almost invariably mention God's support for his kingship, could hardly be faulted if he saw a future for himself in which his memory would be held akin to Joshua's.

Reading the accounts of Athelstan's battle-won glory repeated generation after generation, the importance of Brunanburh is clear.

Almost exactly two years after his victory on the Wirral, Athelstan died in October 939. He chose not to be buried with his father and grandfather in Winchester. Nor, for that matter, did he choose burial beside his aunt Aethelflaed at St Oswald's Priory in Gloucester. Instead, he took his final rest at Malmesbury Abbey, beside his two cousins who had died at Brunanburh. His 18-year-old half-brother, Edmund, who had fought alongside him at that battle, was crowned king.

Anlaf sailed out from Ireland almost immediately. Athelstan had taken York from the Vikings by striking during the tumult of a succession in the city; Anlaf now did the same after the English king's death. He strode into York, seemingly unopposed, and declared himself king of Northumbria. He began to issue coins in his own name. He crossed the Humber, attacking English holdings to the south. After his death in 941, his cousin, Anlaf Sihtricson (often referred to by the Irish name Amlaib Cuaran), took over the throne in York: it was his father's death in 927 that had prompted Athelstan's seizure of the city. If the list of the dead in the *Annals of Clonmacnoise* is to be believed, two of this Anlaf's brothers had died fighting alongside Anlaf Guthfrithson at Brunanburh.[6]

The timeline of events in the 940s isn't consistent across our sources, but it's clear that large swathes of northern England – including parts of the Five Boroughs that the English had wrested from the Vikings – soon fell under York's sway. Athelstan's victory hadn't ended the Viking threat for good. Within a decade, so many of the territorial gains that his family had made were rolled back. Edmund's position was so weakened that sometime in the early 940s he met with one of these same-named rulers of York at Leicester in order to broker a peace. The treaty that was made once more divided England between the English and the Vikings. The line between them would be Watling Street, just as it was in the treaty that Edmund's grandfather Alfred had made with Guthrum a half-century before. These events remind us that Anlaf's Brunanburh campaign hardly needed to have been directly targeted at York – the Vikings had a political claim that reached well beyond that city. What the alliance had failed to manage at Brunanburh had nevertheless come to pass.

Despite the peace made at Leicester, the decades to come would be marked by conflict between these two worlds. King Eadred of England would wrest back control of Northumbria in 954, but even this wasn't the end of Viking political influence in England. The 980s were marked by increasing raids. After the battle of Maldon in 991, King Athelred II the Unready agreed to pay a tribute to the Danish king, called the Danegeld. He nevertheless lost the crown to King Sweyn Forkbeard of Denmark and Norway in 1013. The crown fluctuated between Norse and English hands before it was finally taken away from them both: the English King Harold II Godwinson killed the Norwegian King Harald Hardrada at the battle of Stamford Bridge ... only to be himself killed by the Norman Duke William at the battle of Hastings on 14 October 1066.[7]

These events might seem to diminish Brunanburh. Some might suggest that Brunanburh's reputation is profoundly undeserved, that perhaps the battle's place in our cultural awareness has more to do with its mystery than its impact.

But consider what would have happened if, as nearly occurred, Athelstan had lost.

If the English had been defeated at Brunanburh, if the alliance to topple Athelstan had won, the map of the British Isles would have been irrevocably altered. Something of England might have survived, cobbled together in a moment of despair, as it was in Alfred's day. But it would have been a much smaller England. Athelstan's victory gave the English claim to an extent of land that is recognizable as modern England; his loss would have reduced England into something like the Wessex of old. The new power would have been in the north – the real question being whether it rested in a resurgent and expanded Scotland or a reborn Viking influence in York.

But Athelstan didn't lose. He returned to a throne far stronger than it was when he had ridden out to Brunanburh. By uniting, his enemies had nearly taken him down. But that same alliance meant that in a single stroke he had pushed back multiple rival powers. It wasn't a lasting victory for England, but it was a victory that meant England could last.

Brunanburh wasn't the birthplace of England. The real 'birth' of England was that long lost moment when the first of the future English came ashore. It wasn't much at first, this England-to-be, but it grew. We've traced its infancy. We've traced its childhood as it learned to stand on its own two feet.

At Brunanburh, it came of age.

It's easy to view such a statement in terms of the ground itself: a reflection of the map that Athelstan made, which was undone and then remade after his death. His victory at Brunanburh indeed forged that map, established that precedent. But far more important than the map is what tied together the people who made it. Athelstan had placed the entirety of the Anglo-Saxon kingdoms under one rule. Others before him may have dreamed of it, but Athelstan had made it real. He made – of West Saxons and Mercians and all the rest – an English people.

By the later Middle Ages, only a couple of centuries after what Henry of Huntingdon called 'the greatest of battles',[8] the details of the battle of Brunanburh were fading. It was a marginalization wrought of time and shifting political power structures, but it was never complete. Though its location, its key figures, and even its name were being lost, the perilousness of the moment that Brunanburh represented was never forgotten. In the 14th-century poem *Stanzaic Guy of Warwick*, for instance, King Athelstan faces Anlaf and an alliance that was now an army of Danes and a mighty African giant. With such foes at his gates, the king laments to his parliament at Winchester:

If he overcomes us in battle
he will slay us all without doubt
and destroy all our people.

Then shall England evermore
live in thraldom and in woe
unto the world's end.[9]

Time had brought to long-dead Athelstan a new setting for this greatest of battles, but the threat to England's existence remained the same. Whether imagined as unfolding across the splintered shields and the 'never greater slaughter' of the *Anglo-Saxon Chronicle*, across the field marked by the hazel rods of *Egil's Saga*, or in the relatively humane arrangement of a single combat as in the romantic vision of the *Stanzaic Guy of Warwick* ... the final truth was the same.

In one day, on one field, England came of age.

Appendix

Objections and Alternate Sites

To catalogue and address all the alternative battlefield locations would be a book in itself, but it's worth mentioning a few of the most prominent claimants and why I find them unconvincing.

First, a brief summary of answers to some of the more common objections shared by those who place the battle elsewhere:

COMMON OBJECTIONS

Objection 1. Dingismere doesn't mean 'mere of the Thing' and instead means 'the loud sounding sea'. Language isn't mathematics. Any proposed translation of a problematic word cannot be 100 per cent certain. We are dealing with probabilities no matter which way we go, and it would be irresponsible to claim otherwise. I think the probabilities favour a place-name connected to a Thing, but even if we rejected this reading entirely it doesn't undermine the Wirral claim, which is built on a much larger body of evidence. If *dingismere* refers only to a stormy sea, then its value to *any* proposed location is what I have used it for in this book: an indication that Anlaf's ships were in a sheltered place a short distance from the battlefield, from which they could immediately set out onto the open sea. Wallasey Pool on the Wirral provides exactly this.

Objection 2. That Anlaf isn't recorded returning to Dublin until the following year, Michael Wood says in pitching his most recent alternative site (covered below), 'is an obvious problem if one would place the battle-site on the Mersey, just over a day's sailing from Dublin.'[1] It's true that a day is less than a couple of weeks (the time it would likely take to return from Wood's preferred site off the Humber), but in either case we're well off from many months. Clearly something else is going on. Perhaps our sources just didn't register an earlier return to Ireland. Or, as Wood himself suggests (I think correctly), Anlaf wintered in Scotland, which eliminates the issue altogether: whether it would have taken a day or two weeks to get to Dublin is irrelevant, because Anlaf went to Scotland.

Objection 3. The statement in the *Annals of Clonmacnoise* that the allies gave battle in England with 'the help of the Danes of that kingdom' has been interpreted by many as indicating an allied seizure of York before the battle. Such a reading would require that the contemporary Irish annalist across the sea recognized York as part of 'that kingdom' of England – uncertain to say the least – but it also ignores the evidence of Scandinavian presence elsewhere on the island, such as is known to have existed upon the Wirral and along the Lancashire coast. Any sense that the Brunanburh campaign was engaged in and around York itself has much heavy-lifting to do in explaining why none of our sources mention York in connection with the Brunanburh campaign.

Objection 4. Much warfare before and after Brunanburh took place in the north, so many insist that Brunanburh must therefore be in the north, too. Not so. Athelstan and his immediate predecessors were engaged in combat across nearly every part of what we today call England. And even were they not, this wouldn't inform the location of Brunanburh: as the entire history of warfare shows, a predominance of fighting on one front doesn't preclude fighting on another – especially given the very different motivations of the allied force arranged against the English in 937.

Objection 5. The old poem that William of Malmesbury preserves in his work refers to 'the northern lands' giving support to Anlaf and Constantine, which leads to 'the entire region' yielding to the allies.[2] These references are, for Wood in particular, unambiguous references to a full Northumbrian submission, and he argues that preceding lines underscore this. As he translates them: 'Now the barbarian monster lies on the northern lands (*in terris aquilonis*) / Now quitting the ocean the pirate Anlaf camps on land'.[3] Wood's parenthetical suggests that this translation is straight off the Latin, but it's not. What follows is the Latin, along with the translation of Professor Scott Thompson Smith:

> Iam cubat in terris fera barbaries aquilonis
> Iam iacet in campo pelago pirate relicto
>
> Now the savage barbarity of the north comes to ground,
> now the pirate has left the sea to take the field.[4]

Thus the lines are referring to Anlaf being a Northman (that is, a Viking), not referring to his arrival in any specific place in the north. Wood is right, though, that the poet does say in the later lines that 'the northern lands' supported the grand alliance, and that an 'entire region' yielded to them. It's possible that the 'entire region' is not 'the northern lands', and it's likewise possible that 'the northern lands' are not Northumbria, but I think these possibilities would be unlikely. At the same time, however, it must be remembered that this is a poem characterized by its hyperbole. It is this source that claims Athelstan had 'one hundred thousand soldiers' in his army, and that 'Anlaf, alone of what were recently so many thousands', was the only man to escape the English triumph with his life.[5] The submission of the 'entire region' of 'the northern lands' is surely cut from this same cloth. In the absence of corroboration that the whole of Northumbria physically fell into Anlaf's hands – truly, you would think this would have been bigger news – all we can really conclude from the poem is that there was a number of Northumbrians who supported or even joined the alliance.

This is hardly the same thing as Anlaf seizing York or even aiming for the city. Such support would also be expected no matter where Brunanburh is located. On top of this, we must remind ourselves that even if this poem does indeed date from the tenth century – a point on which there is debate, but upon which I'm very much inclined to agree with Wood – it nevertheless survives only in a clearly modernized 12th-century version from the hand of William of Malmesbury. How much William altered the meaning of the source in this process cannot now be known.

Objection 6. Following along on the previous objection, it has been suggested that numismatics might provide evidence that Anlaf seized Northumbria in 937. In a 1974 study of Athelstan's coinage, Christopher Blunt noted that there are some northern coins that are struck from two reverse dies (that is, they don't have the typical 'front' with the king's name on them): their existence 'prompts the thought that there may have been an occasion when, both at York and at Nottingham, the moneyers deemed it prudent to avoid showing allegiance to the English king, without committing themselves to the other side, and the Viking raid of 937 is an obvious occasion when this might have been the case.'[6] But such political tight-roping is hardly the only explanation for coins like this, much less the most probable one. Typically, double-reversed coins are explained as simple mistakes, which, as Blunt himself says in the next sentence, could well be the case here, too: 'the possibility of error cannot be ruled out'. Erroneous strikes seem especially likely in this instance, since, as Blunt observes when he first comments on the theory that York fell in 937, 'Certainly there is no identifiable break in Athelstan's coinage there and no coins in the name of Anlaf that can be associated with such a capture'.[7] Note that this is quite apart from what happened when Anlaf *did* seize York just a couple years later after Athelstan's death: coinage at that point quickly shifted to reflect the new political rule. In other words, the direct numismatic evidence that would be expected if Northumbria was in non-English hands in 937 does not exist. Indeed, *if* there was reason to insist that some of these coins were double-reversed deliberately rather than mistakenly, then the most obvious explanation would be that this occurred between Athelstan's death and Anlaf's seizure of York. At that point, the local moneyers would have had every reason to be uncertain who was in control of the city and to have minted coins accordingly.

Objection 7. Bromborough isn't recorded in the Domesday Book. William the Conqueror's great survey of 1086 records Eastham ('Estham') as the primary town in the region, with the settlements of Thingwall ('Tuigvelle'), Storeton ('Stortone'), Thornton ('Torintone') and Poulton ('Pontone') surrounding the location of the battle argued here. The absence of a Brunanburh or Bromborough on this list has been said to prove that Bromborough as a local name didn't exist until the 12th century and so, while it may derive from an earlier Brunanburh, it cannot be *the* tenth-century Brunanburh. The problem is that London, Winchester, and Bristol – to name some famous examples – also aren't in the Domesday Book, and we're quite certain they existed. Even on the local Wirral landscape, there are a number of sites, like Overchurch, Bidston, and Birkenhead, that don't appear in Domesday but have archaeological traces of existing at the time. Absence of evidence isn't evidence of absence.

Objection 8. Because the Wirral has the only *Brunanburh* on the map (in modern Bromborough), those seeking the battle elsewhere will often replace this place-name with something that better fits their alternative location for the battle. By far the strongest of these attempts, and thus the one most often cited today, is that of Michael Wood, who now argues that the original form wasn't *Brunanburh* (-*n*-) but was instead *Brunnanburh* (-*nn*-). This would be a multilingual combination of Old Norse *brunnr*, meaning a 'spring' or 'well' with the now-familiar Old English *burh* ('fort').[8] By no small coincidence, this 'fort by the spring' allows Wood to suggest a fit with his latest alternative location for Brunanburh (about which more momentarily) – though in truth a -*nn*- spelling would fit the Wirral location described here, as well as many another site in England. Wood gives sterling effort to his argument, though it problematically ignores the early naming of the site as *Brune* in the *Annales Cambriae*, and his argument that the *-n-* spelling is a southern correction from an unrecognized northern *-nn-* spelling could also be read the other way around: his strongest reason to give preference to the *-nn-* form is that it fits with his preconception of an originally northern battle.

Objection 9. In 1957, the philologist John Dodgson, while arguing that Bromborough derives from Old English *Brunanburh*, nevertheless said that 'it is impossible to connect in any detailed way the facts known about Brunanburh' to the 'context of political and geographical factors' on the Wirral. As a result, some will argue that if we throw out the place-name evidence we have no reason to tie the battle to the Wirral. Although why one would want to throw out the most certain information we have about Brunanburh escapes me, I hope the preceding has shown that the Wirral offers far more than place-name evidence in its favour. The fact that Dodgson didn't recognize it all a half-century ago is irrelevant.

Objection 10. Brunanburh theorists have on occasion dismissed the evidence of one or more of our sources on the basis that the source dated an event incorrectly. Doing so ignores the fact that medieval chronicles in general are notoriously unreliable when it comes to dating. Perhaps entries from one year were mistakenly placed under another, or a copyist might have mistakenly omitted part of a Roman numeral, or an entry was placed into a yearly record when it was heard about instead of when it happened ... the reasons for error can be limitless. The *Annals of Clonmacnoise*, for instance, places the death of Edward the Elder in 920 when it was in 924, and the death of Athelstan in 933 when it was in 939. Its battle on the plains of *othlyn* is dated to 931, which would be either 11 years into Athelstan's reign (and thus in reality 935) or two years before his death (and thus 937). Since the second option equates the battle with Brunanburh, which features the same described personnel in conflict, this seems the logical choice. The need to make such timeline corrections isn't surprising to those who work with these sources. If we start dismissing sources based on dating errors, after all, we would also have to leave out two copies of the vaunted *Anglo-Saxon Chronicle* that originally dated Brunanburh to the wrong year – including the 'A' version with the famous poem!

ALTERNATIVE SITES

Barnsdale Bar. After his previous argument for Brinsworth was found wanting, Michael Wood moved on to make a stronger case for Barnsdale Bar, just north of Doncaster.[9] Wood very rightly observes that several of our early place-names for the battle-site reference a hill, including Aethelweard's *Brunandune* and Symeon of Durham's *Wendune*. The latter is of particular note, Wood suggests, because we can find something similar on the map today in Went Hill, which sits just north of the River Went on the A1 south-west of Castleford. This looks quite promising, not least because the A1 largely follows the western routing of Ermine Street, a Roman road that became the primary conduit between London and York: the majority of military campaigns between the south and north, including Athelstan's earlier march in 934, utilized this very route. Not surprisingly, the road also offers numerous known burhs, including one close to a water source south of Went Hill: a spring called Robin Hood's Well. This, as noted in Objection 8, allows Wood to claim his site checks off the name *Brunanburh*, too.

Wood also sees enormous support for his case in the fact that it fits with John of Worcester's Humber entry and the assumption of a Northumbrian-focused campaign. I have rejected both of these points at some length above. Even if we set these difficulties aside, however, problems remain. Wood is among those keen to point out that while there's no question that Bromborough derives from *brunanburh*, there is no record of the place-name until the 12th century; thus, it cannot be conclusive evidence for the tenth-century battle (Objection 7). Alas, this objection would also mean the erasure of his own Went Hill (which may not derive from *wendune* anyway) as evidence, since *it* isn't recorded until the

12th century either. Likewise, he suggests that the Wirral location doesn't offer a prominent hill adequately comparable to his Went Hill, which rises 150 feet above the Went, some four miles north of his presumed 'burh at the spring': 'there is no such feature near Bromborough', he writes.[10] Yet Storeton Hill, the ridgeline *immediately* beside the site reconstructed here rises just as far above the Brimstage. (Four miles north of the Wirral site, for what it's worth, is Bidston Hill, which would stand 200 feet above the allied ships in Wallasey Pool.) And while it's true that the majority of the campaigns by the English into Northumbria (and vice versa) can be mapped to this road in the decades before and after Brunanburh, that doesn't mean that Brunanburh fits among them (Objection 4). Indeed, the fact that we can map those campaigns so well – and yet we're given no comparable information for the greatest of the period's battles – is a strong indicator that it simply did not happen where all the others did. Why does no source mention mighty York, which must have fallen for Wood's location to make any sense at all? Why would no account of Brunanburh mention the battle's close proximity to Doncaster, which is nearly as close to Robin Hood's Well as the spring is to Went Hill? How could the site of the battle have been forgotten when it was in so well-travelled a spot? Where on such a landscape would we imagine Dingesmere, a location that could fit the landing of the allied fleet and yet also be in reach for the fleeing remnants of the defeated army as night fell?

I *greatly* support Wood's exhortation that historians must keep an 'open mind': we truly must throw alternatives against the wall to see what sticks. I just don't think this one does.

Lanchester. This is the favoured location of Andrew Breeze.[11] It has a Roman road, which is good. It has a hill, which is also good. And it has known fortifications at Roman Longovicium, for which it was named. Breeze, like Wood, accepts John of Worcester's Humber entry without hesitation, which is already highly problematic. For his part, he claims that we know the Humber story is true because John's claim was almost immediately copied by the monk Symeon of Durham, who was writing eight miles away from the 'true' location of Brunanburh at Lanchester and was thus in a position to know. Aside from the logical fallacy here, Symeon of Durham called the site 'Wendune which is called by another name Et Brunnanwerc or Brunnanbyrig'.[12] Thus the monk who was in such a perfect position to affirm Breeze's theory gave us three different names for the location ... but not one of them is Lanchester – which is what the place was always called – or makes any reference to his own nearby Durham.

Burnswark in Dumfriesshire. This prominent hill, north of the Solway Firth, is the preferred site of Kevin Halloran, and it has a number of points very much in its favour.[13] Unlike any 'eastern theory' of the campaign centred on the Humber (the phrase is Halloran's), it's on what I would consider the correct side of Britain. We are also wholly in agreement that the goal of the alliance was not to seize York for Anlaf (as Wood, Breeze, and other Humber theorists insist): it was intended to check if not bury the imperial aims of the English king. We also agree that the battle is ideally situated within a frontier space with mixed linguistic groups, thus accounting not only for our divergent place-names but also for the loss of memory over its exact location. The Roman remains still extant at Burnswark could easily account for the *weorc* on our checklist of names, and the fortifications more generally could be the *burh*. Halloran argues that the hill on which they sit could be the *dun* on our checklist, though it has no greater reason for that claim than any number of other hills across the British Isles. As for the much-needed *brun-* element, Halloran suggests that the Celtic name of the hill referred to its breast-like shape (that shape neatly accounting for the *wen* on our check-list), and this is referenced in the *Pictish Chronicle*'s place-name for the battle, *Duin Brunde*, which he reads as a scribal error for a Gaelic *Dun Bruinde*, meaning 'breast-hill'. Scribes could indeed make such mistakes – I think it likely a copyist error explains the place-name *othlyn* – though it is generally preferable to have more evidence to triangulate such errors. However, even if we accept this proposed scribal snafu, there's little to bridge the further gap between such forms and

Burnswark: the *burn* of *Burnswark* isn't a mistaken *brun*, it's a direct reference to local features like 'Agricola's Well', the natural springs (Old English *burn*) that are the very reason Burnswark was an excellent place for fortified works through the ages.[14] This is already problem enough in my view, but Burnswark is also too far north. Our sources make clear that the battle of Brunanburh took place inside English territory, that Athelstan, as the *Brunanburh* poem puts it, 'defended the land'.[15] Burnswark, on the northern side of Hadrian's Wall, doesn't nearly fit that bill. With so many sources giving us hints of an English march north in 934, a silence on anything similar in 937 is simply deafening: wherever Brunanburh was, it wasn't so far away that anyone remembered a lengthy march through cities and the frontier. Such a far northern location also wouldn't make a lot of sense with what happened in the days after the battle, when Athelstan declined to pursue his enemies: if he had just smashed their armies at Burnswark, the lands of Owain and Constantine would have been open to the very expansionist impulse that the allies had sought to contain.

Suggested Reading and Acknowledgements

A number of books lived on my desk as I wrote this book. Sarah Foot's *Æthelstan* (Yale University Press, 2012) is a truly fantastic biography of the king who won at Brunanburh and is a must-read. It combines well with Paul Hill's *The Age of Athelstan* (Tempus, 2004). Those wanting a briefer but still solid account of the man should seek out Tom Holland's *Athelstan* (Allen Lane, 2016), though I disagree with the extent to which he pitches Brunanburh as a religious fight. Clare Downham, in her truly superb *Viking Kings of Britain and Ireland* (Dunedin, 2007), marvellously clarifies the tangled web of political, military, and family dynamics that surround the Ivar dynasty and the North Sea. The Scots perspective on this same period is available through the wonderful *From Pictland to Alba, 789-1070* (Edinburgh University Press, 2007), by Alex Woolf. Decades after its initial publication, Alfred P. Smyth's *Scandinavian York and Dublin* (Irish Academic, 1987) remains a standard reference for the interplay of these two Viking kingdoms.

The rise and impact of King Alfred the Great has been the subject of many books, but the ones I've gone to the most have been Richard Abels' *Alfred the Great* (Longman, 1998) and Ryan Lavelle's *Alfred's Wars* (Boydell Press, 2010). Along with these, Paul Hill's *The Anglo-Saxons at War 800–1066* (Pen and Sword, 2012) is an approachable and useful look at warfare of the period. Nicolas Higham has authored several works that will interest those who enjoyed this book, including *The Kingdom of Northumbria, AD 350–1100* (Alan Sutton, 1993) and, as a fascinating approach to early medieval Britain, *King Arthur: The Making of a Legend* (Yale University Press, 2018). So much of what is known about the history of Owain's kingdom comes from Tim Clarkson's *Strathclyde and the Anglo-Saxons in the Viking Age* (John Donald, 2014).

Those wanting to access the original sources should look once again at *The Battle of Brunanburh: A Casebook*, ed. Michael Livingston (Exeter/Liverpool University Press, 2011): it has the source evidence in the original languages and translations that will empower agreement or disagreement with the Wirral case that is argued in several (but not all) of the accompanying essays in the volume. It also provides the bibliography for accessing those sources for coverage beyond the battle itself. I'll note here, as well, that my favourite one-volume translation of the different versions of the *Anglo-Saxon Chronicle* is that of Michael Swanton (J.M. Dent, 1996). The *Annals of Ulster* and other Irish sources are available online (in English translation and in their original languages) through the enormously beneficial CELT project housed at University College Cork (https://celt.ucc.ie/index.html).

* * *

I've been extraordinarily fortunate to have a strong network of colleagues, friends, and family that supported me in writing this book. Myke Cole is as excellent a first-reader as he is a writer himself. This book is in every way better thanks to him. Kelly DeVries saved me from more than one embarrassing mistake as he likewise went through my draft. Robert Woosnam-Savage was a source of tremendous insights when we journeyed to look at Wirral Archaeology's initial findings. At home, Kayla, Samuel, and Elanor have kept my ship riding on an even keel no matter the storms of life. I cannot thank them all enough.

This book would never have happened were it not for all those involved in the *Brunanburh Casebook*, especially Paul Cavill, Richard Coates, and Stephen Harding, whose triumvirate of essays are a gold-mine. Peter Konieczny's suggestion that I write a larger reconstruction of the battle using *Egil's Saga* turned out to be sufficient provocation to write a book, for which I'm grateful. My agent, Paul Stevens, was enormously patient in stepping out of his comfort zone to shop the idea, and I'm glad Marcus Cowper at Osprey took the call, and that he was so brilliantly assisted in the book's production by Gemma Gardner. The good folks at Wirral Archaeology were a constant inspiration to the project with their ongoing work in the fields where we believed the battle happened. More than that, several members served as conduits of information and eyes on the ground after the pandemic put an unexpected hold on my research travels. I thank them all, but particular shout-outs go to Graham Burgess, Pete Jenkins, Peter France, and Brian Griffiths for answering my emails and acting as my eyes on the ground when the pandemic had me grounded. Pete Holder, you're a great drone pilot.

I owe thanks to Wirhahl Skip Felagr for their infectious enthusiasm, and to Richard Cutts of Mad Mylo Photography for orchestrating photos of a remarkable gathering of re-enactors, esteemed WSF members all: Steve Banks, Dave Capener, Andrew Quick, Jacob Quick, and Chris Addison.

I'm happy to single out Capener, a member of both Wirral Archaeology and Wirhahl Skip Felagr, for his *enormous* generosity in sharing with me his unpublished 'Brunanburh Battlefield Assessment'. While I've noted my disagreement with a few of his positions, these are niggling details against the larger commonality that we have in where we place the battle. Seeing that his independent conclusions matched mine was an absolute relief!

The Wirral Borough Council graciously allowed me to communicate with Paul Sherman of PHC Services regarding their initial assessment report on Wirral Archaeology's project. Paul then provided some excellent photography of the artefacts, along with his up-to-date professional analysis of them. Another of the authors of that report, Clare Downham, provided kind words at a time when I needed them – to go along with the priceless gift of her aforementioned scholarship.

'No one has done more than Michael Livingston to revive memories of the battle', Bernard Cornwell writes in the foreword to this book. I confess I'm still stunned by it, especially in light of the many names listed above. With respect, though, I'd suggest he has it quite precisely backwards: no one has done more to bring life to Brunanburh than Bernard Cornwell. This book, if I'm enormously lucky, will sell in the thousands. His Saxon Stories series of novels has sold in the millions – to say nothing of the further legions of fans who watch the television adaptation of the books, *The Last Kingdom*. For years, Cornwell's fans (of which I am one) have followed Uhtred of Bebbanburg on a path winding through the rise and fall of kings, crossing the ebb and flow of Viking armies. The 2020 publication of the 13th book, *War Lord*, has now brought Uhtred to the bloody field at Brunanburh. Cornwell's vision of the battle will forever impact the way Brunanburh is remembered, *and rightly so*. My final thanks, then, go to him: for his generosity in writing such a kind foreword to this book … and for his generosity in giving the world his magnificent vision of the 'never greater slaughter' that made England what it is today.

Endnotes

FOREWORD

1 *The Battle of Brunanburh: A Casebook*, ed. Michael Livingston (Liverpool University Press, 2011; hereafter known as *Brunanburh Casebook*), p. 1.
2 Ibid., trans. Michael Livingston, 4a.65–68 (translation slightly revised).
3 Ibid., trans. Michael Livingston, 4a.5.

PREFACE

1 This is the definition put forth by Clare Downham in *Viking Kings of Britain and Ireland* (Dunedin, 2007), p. xvi, a book that cannot be more highly recommended for its comprehensive look at this period.

INTRODUCTION

1 *The Battle of Crécy: A Casebook*, ed. Michael Livingston and Kelly DeVries (Liverpool University Press, 2015), trans. Elizaveta Strakhov, 3.525–33.
2 The various manuscript copies of the *Anglo-Saxon Chronicle* are sufficiently different that they are typically labelled as 'versions' by scholars. The *Brunanburh* poem thus appears in Versions A (sometimes also called the Winchester or Parker Chronicle), B (the Abingdon Chronicle I), C (the Abingdon Chronicle II), and D (the Worcester Chronicle). Versions E and F omit the poem in favour of short notices of the battle. Quotations from the chronicle here and elsewhere are taken from Version A unless otherwise specified.
3 *Brunanburh Casebook*, trans. Michael Livingston, 4a.60–70.

4 Ibid., trans. Michael Livingston, 4a.31.

5 *Egil's Saga*, trans. Bernard Scudder, in *The Sagas of the Icelanders*, ed. Örnólfur Thorsson (Viking, 2000), p. 90.

6 The gift of poetry was in the form of a special mead, brewed from a dead god's blood, that Odin in the form of an eagle had flown across the Nine Worlds of Creation to retrieve. As he carried it in his mouth, some of this mead spilled out, diluted with his own spit, while still other parts he swallowed and urinated as he flew – such could explain the very worst to the literally piss-poor mediocre poetry of the world. The finest poets, though, drank of the pure mead from the mouth of Odin, father-god.

7 This section of *Egil's Saga* (Chapter 55) is not printed in the *Brunanburh Casebook*. For the original text in context with other works of the period, see *The Longman Anthology of Old English, Old Icelandic and Anglo-Norman Literatures*, ed. Richard North, Joe Allard and Patricia Gilles (Longman, 2011), p. 652.

8 I've left this term untranslated here since, as a place-name, it is one of our clues to finding the location of Brunanburh. Such terms will be discussed later in the book.

9 For the original text, see *The Longman Anthology*, p. 652.

10 For the original text, see ibid., p. 654.

11 For the original text, see ibid.

12 *Brunanburh Casebook*, trans. A. Keith Kelly, 25.259–66.

13 Ibid., trans. A. Keith Kelly, 25.68–69.

14 *The Battle of Crécy: A Casebook*, trans. Kelly DeVries, 60.181–85.

CHAPTER 1 THE BIRTH OF ENGLAND, TO 865

1 'For the sun gave forth its light without brightness, like the moon, during the whole year'; Procopius, *History of the Wars* 4.14.

2 *Medieval Warfare: A Reader*, ed. Kelly DeVries and Michael Livingston (University of Toronto Press, 2019), pp. xiii-xiv.

3 Zosimus, *Historia Nova* 6.10.2.

4 Zosimus' history stops just weeks before the sack of Rome. From the context of Zosimus' work, which has all the chronological clarity of mud, E.A. Thompson has argued – and I think settled the matter – that *if* the letters from Honorius really existed then they would have been written in June. See E.A. Thompson, 'Zosimus 6. 10. 2 and the Letters of Honorius', *The Classical Quarterly* 32.2 (1982), p. 451.

5 Zosimus, 6.5.3.
6 See, for example, St Patrick's discussion of his own life in his
   autobiography of the period, where he refers to no great social or
   political upheaval at all.
7 Gildas, *The Ruin of Britain*, ed. and trans. Michael Winterbottom
   (Phillimore, 1978), §14.
8 Ibid., §23.
9 Ibid., §24.
10 Ibid., §26.

CHAPTER 2 THE VIKINGS ARRIVE, 837–66

1 For a summary of the context of the debate and this more recent
   position, which was first put forward by David Dumville, see
   Downham, *Viking Kings*, pp. xv–xviii.
2 Donnchadh Ó Corráin, 'The Vikings in Scotland and Ireland in the
   Ninth Century', *Chronicon* 2 (1998), 3.1–45.
3 It remains uncertain, however, just how hard a line the Irish would
   have drawn between *any* of these overseas entities. It's almost surely
   the case that there was a Viking kingdom north of the Irish Sea. It
   seems likely that it was called *Lochlann*, and that it was the immediate
   source of the 'dark' foreigners. But from the Irish perspective they
   could just as well have seen *Lochlann* as also extending across the
   North Sea to the ancestral homeland of the Viking threat. This
   would explain how the term over time became more focused to
   refer, as it does today, specifically to Norway.
4 The *Fragmentary Annals* are, like so many of our sources, problematic.
   Scholars believe that the source text dates from the middle of the
   11th century, but it only survives in a 17th-century copy now held
   at the Bibliothèque Royale in Brussels.
5 There are theories, though, among them that 'Boneless' could mean
   that he was legless or otherwise handicapped ... or that he was
   sexually impotent!
6 *Anglo-Saxon Chronicle*, E.787.

CHAPTER 3 ALFRED AND THE VIKING CONQUEST, 866–99

1 For the original Old English and an alternative translation to mine,
   see *The Longman Anthology*, pp. 269–72.

2 For the original Old Norse, see *Knútsdrapa* 1 in *Poetry from the Kings' Sagas 1: From Mythical Times to c. 1035*, ed. Diana Whaley, Skaldic Poetry of the Scandinavian Middle Ages 1 (Brepols, 2012), p. 651.

3 The original Old Norse is in *Þáttr af Ragnars Sonum*, ed. Guðni Jónsson and Bjarni Vilhjálmsson (Bókaútgáfan Forni, 1943–44), Chapter 3.

4 By comparison, the practice of quartering a fallen enemy – cutting the body into pieces and sending the parts into various districts as a warning – is so well documented that we have an accountant-styled receipt of the costs involved from the quartering of Hotspur after the battle of Shrewsbury in 1403.

5 *The Anglo-Saxon Chronicle*, trans. and ed. M.J. Swanton (Routledge, 1998), p. 70 (A.870).

6 The treaty doesn't set Guthrum's northern border, which would have run against the kingdom of Strathclyde around Morecambe Bay and the holdings of English Northumbria, with its capital in Bamburgh, which began around the River Tees. It was also quickly clear that even this southern border was fluid.

7 *Anglo-Saxon Chronicle*, p. 72 (A.874).

8 Patrick Wormald, 'Making of England', *History Today* 45.2 (1995), p. 26.

9 In this discussion, I am indebted to Guy Halsall, 'Playing by Whose Rules? A Further Look at Viking Atrocity in the Ninth Century', *Medieval History* 2.2 (1992), 2–12.

10 Ecclesiastes 9:11.

CHAPTER 4 THE GATHERING STORM, 900–24

1 *The Annals of Ulster to AD 1131*, ed. and trans. Seán Mac Airt & Gearóid Mac Niocaill (Dublin Institute for Advanced Studies, 1983), U873.3.

2 Ibid., U902.2.

3 The *Anglo-Saxon Chronicle*'s report that the Vikings took a 'deserted city in the Wirral that is called Chester' (A.894) has led many to assume that the city had been abandoned for some time, but this ignores the possibility that it might have been temporarily or just partially abandoned as the Vikings approached. Far from being long deserted, there was enough significant economic activity in the area to support a mint from around the year 890.

4 *Fragmentary Annals of Ireland*, ed. and trans. Joan Newlon Radner (Dublin Institute for Advanced Studies, 1978), §429.
5 Alex Woolf, *From Pictland to Alba, 789–1070* (Edinburgh University Press, 2007), p. 141.
6 *Historia de sancto Cuthberto*, ed. and trans. Ted Johnson South (Cambridge University Press, 2002), §22, pp. 60–61.
7 For quite some time, it was thought that there were *two* battles of Corbridge: one in 914 and one in 918. This position was conclusively refuted by Woolf, *From Pictland to Alba*, pp. 143–44.
8 *Anglo-Saxon Chronicle*, p. 104 (A.923).

CHAPTER 5   THE RISE OF ATHELSTAN, 924–34

1 In her excellent biography of Athelstan, Sarah Foot has neatly demonstrated that the evidence within William's text – including his unique stories and the apparent language of the verses that he says he is translating – strongly indicates 'that William had succeeded in finding a unique source of information about the king's reign'; *Æthelstan*, (Yale University Press, 2012), p. 258.
2 Foot, *Æthelstan*, p. 75. Athelstan wasn't the first to use such a title. His grandfather, Alfred the Great, had invented the title *Anglorum-Saxonum rex*, 'king of the Anglo-Saxons', in the late 880s.
3 Michael Lapidge, 'Some Latin Poems as Evidence for the Reign of Athelstan', *Anglo-Saxon England* 9 (1981), pp. 72–73. I'm fully convinced by Foot's dismantling of Lapidge's argument that the poem be dated to Alfred's presentation to his grandson; it makes far more sense as an expression of hope for an adult's immediate reign than for a young child's unknown future. Still uncertain is the question of whether 'John' is the name of the poet, as Lapidge has argued, or a secondary name of the king, as Foot has argued (*Æthelstan*, pp. 33, 110–12).
4 For the original Latin and an alternative translation to mine, see William of Malmesbury, *De gestis regum Anglorum I*, ed. and trans. R.A.B. Mynors, R.M. Thomson and M. Winterbottom (Oxford University Press, 1998), 2.135, pp. 218–21.
5 For an excellent run-down of the gifts and their likely origins, see Foot, *Æthelstan*, pp. 192–98.
6 G.A. Kornbluth, *Engraved Gems of the Carolingian Empire* (Pennsylvania State University Press, 1995), plate 14.
7 *Anglo-Saxon Chronicle*, p. 107 (D.926).

8 There are good reasons to doubt that this expedition into Cornwall was quite as William imagines it. For an overview, see Foot, *Æthelstan*, p. 164.

9 Most scholars have assumed that the poet was from the Continent, but his use of the Latin *Saxonia* for England could also leave open the possibility that he hailed from Wales.

10 *Brunanburh Casebook*, trans. Michael Lapidge, 2.10–20.

11 *Annals of Clonmacnoise*, ed. Denis Murphy (Dublin, 1896), p. 149 (s.a. 928 [for 933/34]); *Annals of Ulster*, U934.1.

CHAPTER 6 THE GREAT ALLIANCE, 934–37

1 *Brunanburh Casebook*, trans. John K. Bollard, 1.8–16.

2 Ibid., trans. John K. Bollard, 1.27–30 and 1.40–43.

3 Ibid., trans. John K. Bollard, 1.53–68.

4 Ibid., trans. John K. Bollard, 1.186–87.

5 Ibid., trans. Scott Thompson Smith, 13.3.

6 Ibid., trans. Michael Livingston, 9.3, 12.2.

7 Ibid., trans. A. Keith Kelly, 25.1.

CHAPTER 7 RECONSTRUCTING BATTLES

1 Edward Hallett Carr, *What Is History? The George Macaulay Trevelyan Lectures Delivered at the University of Cambridge January–March 1961* (Vintage Books, 1961), p. 16.

2 John of Worcester, *The Chronicle of John of Worcester, Volume II: The Annals from 450–1066*, ed. and trans. R.R. Darlington and P. McGurk (Oxford University Press, 1995), p. 486 [s.a. 1016].

3 Richard Abels and Stephen Morillo, 'A Lying Legacy? A Preliminary Discussion of Images of Antiquity and Altered Reality in Medieval Military History', *Journal of Medieval Military History* 3 (2005), pp. 2–4.

CHAPTER 8 THE SEARCH FOR BRUNANBURH

1 Shakespeare, *Henry V*, 4.3.47–53.

2 As historian Ryan Lavelle puts it when talking about warfare in the period, 'A battle can often be as much a construction of succeeding generations as it is the achievement of the generation who fought it'. *Alfred's Wars: Anglo-Saxon Warfare in the Viking Age* (Boydell Press, 2010), p. 298.

3 On Hastings, which might well be lost beneath the town of Battle itself, see Michael Livingston and Kelly DeVries, *1066: A Guide to the Battles and the Campaigns* (Pen and Sword, 2020), pp. 164–67. Crécy is traditionally situated north of the town of Crécy, but I think it more likely three and a half miles south near the town of Domvast beside the Forest of Crécy; see Michael Livingston, 'The Location of the Battle of Crécy', in *The Battle of Crécy: A Casebook*, pp. 415–38. And Agincourt, rather than taking place on the flat ground east of the town of Azincourt where wooden figures of archers today line the road, may have run across the hills and a shallow valley just south-west of the town for which it was named; see Michael Livingston, 'Where Was Agincourt Fought?' *Medieval Warfare Magazine* 9.1 (2019), 20–33.

4 Or, more correctly said, names for a battle that we presume is Brunanburh; this is the case with *Egil's Saga*, for instance, which will be discussed below.

5 *Brunanburh Casebook*, trans. Scott Thompson Smith, 16.1–4.

6 As Paul Cavill concludes in his own dismissal of it, 'John misunderstands the Old English poem, confuses personnel, and regards the Humber as the point of entry typically used by northern forces. All these factors make it reasonable to doubt that John has the only accurate tradition about Brunanburh and that all the others omitted such a useful detail' (*Brunanburh Casebook*, p. 339).

7 Ketel's original work has unfortunately been lost, but a later copy of it exists that is assumed to be generally accurate. Because it has nothing to do with Brunanburh, this source is not in the *Brunanburh Casebook*. It was edited by James Raine as *Vita S. Iohannis Eboracensis archiepiscopi* in *The Historians of the Church of York and its Archbishops*, Rolls Series 71.1 (Longman, 1879), pp. 293–320.

8 This kind of votive offering was common all the way back to the ancient period: a sign of devotion in hopes and/or in gratitude to god (or the gods) for a safe return from battle.

9 *Brunanburh Casebook*, trans. Michael Livingston, 36.25–41, 74–84.

10 *Ibid.*, trans. Scott Thompson Smith, 11.2–3.

11 For more in-depth discussion of the alternatives and why these are very likely to be the meanings, see Paul Cavill's terrific breakdown of the elements in the *Brunanburh Casebook*, pp. 331–37.

12 Also lost is the original manuscript of Conall's translation, though copies of it have thankfully been preserved in the British Library and in the Library of Trinity College Dublin.

13 Nicholas Higham, 'The Context of Brunanburh', in *Names, Places and People: An Onomastic Miscellany for John McNeal Dodgson*, ed. Alexander R. Rumble and A.D. Mills (Paul Watkins, 1997), p. 152 n. 66; see also the summary of this position by Cavill in *Brunanburh Casebook*, pp. 346–47.

14 See the *Annals of Clonmacnoise*, p. 148 (s.a. 922 [for 927]). Other *Dublyn* spellings appear in his entries for 897 (p. 144), 971 (p. 158), and 1147 (p. 201).

15 See Paul Cavill, Stephen E. Harding, and Judith Jesch, 'Revisiting *Dingesmere*', *Journal of the English Place-Name Society* 36 (2003/04), 25–38, as well as Cavill's later 'Coming Back to *Dingesmere*', in *Language and Contact in the Place-Names of Britain and Ireland*, ed. Paul Cavill and George Broderick (English Place-Name Society, 2007), 27–41. In addition to this positive argument, Cavill and his colleagues make a negative argument: that theories about the term meaning 'noisy' (thus giving us something like 'noisy sea') cannot hold up to scrutiny; see the *Brunanburh Casebook*, pp. 336–37.

16 Paul Cavill presents an accessible overview of this work in a powerful essay: not only does he make a strong case that *Bromborough* came from *Brunanburh*, but he dismantles any chance that the most common alternative locations for the battle could likewise claim such a clear linguistic connection ('The Place-Name Debate', *Brunanburh Casebook*, pp. 327–49).

17 See Richard Coates, 'The Sociolinguistic Context of Brunanburh', and Stephen Harding, 'Wirral: Folklore and Locations', *Brunanburh Casebook*, pp. 365–83, and 351–63, respectively. Harding's narrowing down of the battle-site matches that of two early 20th-century historians, though reached for entirely different reasons

18 When Overchurch ('church of the shore') was demolished in 1887, an early medieval runic stone was found bearing an inscription soliciting prayers for Aethelmund; there are indications that the hill was previously the site of a lost pre-Christian henge.

19 *Brunanburh Casebook*, p. 21.

CHAPTER 9 THE SHIPS AND THE SAGA

1 *Brunanburh Casebook*, trans. Michael Livingston, 4a.31, 65–66.
2 Ibid., trans. Scott Thompson Smith, 8.2.
3 Ibid., trans. Scott Thompson Smith, 11.2.

4 Ibid., trans. Scott Thompson Smith, 17.25, 32–33.

5 Ibid., trans. Michael Livingston, 52.8–10.

6 Ibid., trans. Scott Thompson Smith, 13.3 and 20.1. In the 13th century, the metrical chronicle of Peter of Langtoft tells us that it was 715 ships, probably garbling this information (*Brunanburh Casebook*, trans. Michael Livingston, 36.77).

7 In the *Brunanburh Casebook* I thus suggested that the Scots might have marched to the Wirral (pp. 17–18). This was asinine, and it has rightly been taken to task on the grounds that such a march would have been difficult and raises significant questions about the campaign. Why, for instance, would the allies 'back up' into the Wirral?

8 *Brunanburh Casebook*, trans. Michael Livingston, 4a.25–32.

9 Ibid., trans. Michael Livingston, 4a.22–23.

10 Ibid., trans. Michael Livingston, 4a.32–36, 37.

11 Ibid., trans. Michael Livingston, 4a.47.

12 Ibid., trans. Michael Livingston, 4a.35, 53.

13 Dave Capener ('Brunanburh Battlefield Assessment' [unpublished, 2020], p. 5) suggests 6,000 men, while Clare Downham has suggested the range here, while favouring the higher end of the scale ('How Big Was the Battle of Brunanburh?', *Academia.edu*, p. 5). I differ significantly with Capener on the number of ships involved: Capener claims 80–100, but this is in part due to his assumption that the ships involved averaged upwards of 100 men each. I imagine far less given the supplies and the need to keep all the vessels seaworthy, but for all we know, he could well be right!

14 Harding, 'Wirral: Folklore and Locations', *Brunanburh Casebook*, p. 359.

15 Capener ('Brunanburh Battlefield Assessment', p. 5) estimates 100 ships, which could shorten the beachfront considerably, though even 1,000 yards of beach would still be rather problematic given what follows.

16 My thanks to Pete Jenkins of Wirral Archaeology for pointing out the sight-lines in this area.

17 See 'Wirral Watersheds and River Systems and Their Influence of Local History', *Transactions of the Historical Society of Lancashire and Cheshire* 74 (1922), p. 127.

18 W. M. Massie, 'On a Wooden Bridge, Found Buried Fourteen Feet Deep Under the Silt at Birkenhead', *Journal of the Chester Archaeological Society* 1 (1857), 55–60.

19 This is the view of Capener ('Brunanburh Battlefield Assessment', p. 19).

20 Harding, 'Wirral: Folklore and Locations', in *Brunanburh Casebook*, pp. 357–58.

21 *Brunanburh Casebook*, trans. A. Keith Kelly, 25.31–38.

22 Ibid., trans. A. Keith Kelly, 25.55–57.

23 On the larger implications of this in warfare, see Guy Halsall, 'Anthropology and the Study of Pre-Conquest Warfare and Society: The Ritual War in Anglo-Saxon England,' in *Weapons and Warfare in Anglo-Saxon England*, ed. S.C. Hawkes (Oxford University Committee for Archaeology Monograph 21, 1989), 155–77.

24 *Brunanburh Casebook*, trans. A. Keith Kelly, 25.143–46.

25 Ibid., trans. A. Keith Kelly, 25.209–10.

26 Ibid., trans. A. Keith Kelly, 25.243–44.

27 For an excellent overview of this, see A. Keith Kelly's essay, 'Truth and a Good Story', in *Brunanburh Casebook*, pp. 305–14.

CHAPTER 10 THE DAY ENGLAND CAME OF AGE, 937

1 *Brunanburh Casebook*, trans. Scott Thompson Smith, 17.14–19.

2 Ibid., trans. Scott Thompson Smith, 17.25–26.

3 This last possibility was among those things that a common freeman must own in order to be considered worthy of becoming a thegn (nobility). Other necessities, according to the Old English legal tract usually entitled *Geþyncðu* (Dignities), which was written between 1008 and 1014, include five hides of land and a bell-house, and a burh-gate. For a classic discussion, see Ann Williams, 'A Bell-house and a Burh-geat', in *Anglo-Norman Castles*, ed. Robert Liddiard (Boydell Press, 2003), p. 74.

4 *Brunanburh Casebook*, p. 345.

5 Depending on the situation, Roman road-builders could also pave a ford, as they did in a surviving example at Iden Green in Kent.

6 I am grateful to Andy Quick of the Wirhall Skip Felagr for testing this out in experimental re-enactment.

7 This alternative is that of Dave Capener, whose work is gratefully acknowledged.

8 *Brunanburh Casebook*, trans. Michael Livingston, 4a.1–20.

9 Ibid., trans. Michael Livingston, 4a.20–56.

10 Francis W.T. Tudsbery, *Brunanburh A.D. 937* (Oxford University Press, 1907), pp. 23–24.

11 Capener, 'Brunanburh Battlefield Assessment', p. 21.
12 *Brunanburh Casebook*, trans. Michael Livingston, 4a.60–73.
13 Ibid., trans. Michael Livingston, 4a.7–10.
14 Ibid., trans. Scott Thompson Smith, 18.23.
15 Ibid., trans. Scott Thompson Smith, 17.3–4.

CHAPTER 11 WIRRAL ARCHAEOLOGY

1 Graham Burgess, personal communication, 16 October 2020.
2 For this and all other detailed analysis of the artefacts, I am indebted to the analysis of Paul Sherman and PHC Services, given by personal communication, 19 October 2020.
3 Michael Livingston, 'An Army on the March and in Camp – Guillaume Guiart's *Branche des royaus lingnages*', *Journal of Medieval Military History* 17 (2019), 269–71.
4 *Brunanburh Casebook*, pp. 354–55.

CHAPTER 12 ENGLAND, COME OF AGE

1 David N. Dumville, *Wessex and England from Alfred to Edgar: Six Essays in Political, Cultural and Ecclesiastical Revival* (Boydell Press, 1992), p. 171.
2 *Brunanburh Casebook*, trans. Scott Thompson Smith, 3.1–6.
3 Joshua 10:24.
4 *Brunanburh Casebook*, trans. Michael Livingston, 4a.28–30.
5 E.g. *Brunanburh Casebook*, trans. Michael Livingston, 10.9, trans. Scott Thompson Smith, 11.23–24.
6 Ibid., trans. Michael Livingston, 52.6.
7 Ironically, this could be viewed as a final victory for the Viking side: the Normans traced their descent from Rollo, a Viking leader who died only a few years before Brunanburh.
8 *Brunanburh Casebook*, trans. Scott Thompson Smith, 18.13.
9 Ibid., trans. Michael Livingston, 37.2863–68.

APPENDIX: OBJECTIONS AND ALTERNATE SITES

1 Michael Wood, 'Searching for Brunanburh: The Yorkshire Context of the "Great War" of 937', *Yorkshire Archaeological Journal* 85 (2013), p. 144.
2 *Brunanburh Casebook*, trans. Scott Thompson Smith, 17.9, 17.11.

3 Wood, 'Searching for Brunanburh', p. 153.

4 *Brunanburh Casebook*, trans. Scott Thompson Smith, 17.5–6.

5 Ibid., trans. Scott Thompson Smith, 17.25, 17.32.

6 C.E. Blunt, 'The Coinage of Athelstan, 924–939: A Survey', *British Numismatic Journal* 44 (1974), p. 92.

7 Ibid., p. 89.

8 Michael Wood, 'The Spelling of Brunanburh', *Notes and Queries* 64.3 (2017), 365–69.

9 For Barnsdale Bar, see his 'Searching for Brunanburh'. His case for Brinsworth is made in 'Brunanburh Revisited', *Saga-Book of the Viking Society* 20 (1980), 200–17, and *In Search of England: Journeys into the English Past* (Penguin, 2000), pp. 206–14.

10 Wood, 'Searching for Brunanburh', p. 146 n. 48.

11 Andrew C. Breeze, 'Brunanburh Located: The Battlefield and the Poem', in *Aspects of Medieval English Language and Literature: Proceedings of the Fifth International Conference of the Society of Historical English Language and Linguistics*, ed. Michiko Ogura and Hans Sauer (Peter Lang, 2018), 61–81.

12 *Brunanburh Casebook*, trans. Scott Thompson Smith, 13.2.

13 Kevin Halloran, 'The Brunanburh Campaign: A Reappraisal', *The Scottish Historical Review* 84.2 (2005), 133–48.

14 For a detailed rebuttal of this location, see Paul Cavill, 'The Battle of Brunanburh in 937: Battlefield Despatches', in *In Search of Vikings: Interdisciplinary Approaches to the Scandinavian Heritage of North-West England*, ed. Stephen E. Harding, David Griffiths, and Elizabeth Royles (CRC Press, 2014), 95–108.

15 *Brunanburh Casebook*, trans. Michael Livingston, 4a.9.

Index